Redemptive Love

Redemptive Love is a fascinating story of a woman who grew up with an alcoholic father and trusted Christ when she was forty-one years old. It is a story of God's amazing and sovereign grace.

–JERRY BRIDGES, author, *The Pursuit of Holiness*

In *Redemptive Love* Claudia Loopstra takes the reader on a fascinating odyssey from her childhood to becoming a committed woman of God. She does not "sugar-coat" her journey, but rather presents us with all of real-world problems that confront so many in our time. This is a story of the triumph of grace in the lives of sinners and of some of the very hard and harsh realities that confront mankind. You will laugh, cry, be angry and rejoice as you read the pages of Claudia's pilgrimage.

–DR. RON GLEASON, preacher/author

A truly inspirational and moving read! Claudia takes us on a journey through her life that touches the full range of human emotion. She shares her traumas and challenges as well as her achievements and victories as we witness her psychological and spiritual development. These two elements are intricately intertwined and propel her forward on the road to self-growth and healing.

–DR. DEBORAH NIXON, psychologist

It took courage to live this story and courage to write it. Claudia has opened up a dark secret to reveal a more beautiful secret only God could show her.

—**HILARY PRICE,** international speaker/author

Redemptive Love is a wonderful, deeply personal story of the power of God to transform lives with the gospel of Jesus Christ. Claudia Loopstra's transparency over sensitive and painful family issues should provide a sense of hope for any reader with relational struggles. The story is a reminder and an encouragement that God has life in his firm grip. He has the last word and can make fine wine out of dirty water. This is a well written and captivating story and a worthwhile read for anyone.

—**REV. JOHN ANDERSON,** PCA pastor

"We went through fire and through water, yet you have brought us to a place of abundance." This testimony of the psalmist could just as easily as be that of Claudia Loopstra, who, in this deeply moving account of her early years, reveals God's sovereign mercy and goodness over all her ways. Personally I love to read of how God has worked in other peoples' lives: despite challenging circumstances, it can be so encouraging and comforting to see God at work. And the story of Claudia's early life has rich food for our encouragement. Highly recommended!

—**DR. MICHAEL A.G. HAYKIN,** historian, author and professor

Redemptive Love is an easy, captivating read as a troubled, confused daughter swings open the door of her heart and welcomes us in. As Claudia, "a wounded healer," courageously shares her strained and painful relationship with her alcoholic father, we are taken down an honest path of pain and sorrow that leads to hope and healing.

—**HEATHER TOMPKINS,** bereavement chaplain

Redemptive Love

Living with an alcoholic father

Claudia Loopstra

joshua
press

www.joshuapress.com

Published by
Joshua Press Inc., Kitchener, Ontario, Canada
Distributed by
Sola Scriptura Ministries International
www.sola-scriptura.ca

Cover and book design by Janice Van Eck
All images courtesy of the author.

Library and Archives Canada Cataloguing in Publication

Loopstra, Claudia, 1944–, author
      Redemptive love : living with an alcoholic father / Claudia Loopstra.

ISBN 978-1-894400-68-8 (paperback)

      1. Loopstra, Claudia, 1944–. 2. Adult children of alcoholics—Canada—Biography. I. Title.

HV5132.L66 2015   362.292'4092   C2015-905118-5

To my grandchildren
Jocelyn, Willem, Graham, Alexandra, Emilie & Taryn

Preface

The following story has been written based on my recollections of how the events in my life unfolded. Dialogue was created to convey how individuals tended to communicate. Some names of peripheral characters have been changed out of respect for their privacy. To the best of my ability, I have been as historically accurate as possible.

Acknowledgements

Thank you to the many people who encouraged me during the writing of my story. With gratitude, I thank my husband, Chuck, who supported me throughout. I would also like to thank him for the unconditional love he always exhibited toward my father and also the way he loved my mother and became like a son to her.

Melinda and Cameron, my two children, I thank you for contributing to my story in a most significant way.

I would like to express appreciation to my writers' group, Friends in the Word: Marguerite Cummings, Glenda Dekkema, Carol Ford and Melony Teague. You kept me motivated and offered up continued prayers. Carol Ford, you spent countless hours supporting me in ways too numerous to mention.

Much appreciation is extended to my great niece, Jennifer Colautti, who began reading this work chapter by chapter at its inception, and for offering her editing skills throughout. Carol Campbell, Mary Sandusky and Heather Tompkins—thank you for your support.

Sally and Ron Gleason, I am indebted to you for teaching me biblical truths. God brought you into my life at just the right time. I value your friendship and your wisdom.

To my editor Patricia Elford, you travelled down this sometimes challenging road with me and brought insight into some of the darker corners of my world.

Joshua Press, thank you for believing in my story and for being the vehicle by which this story will hopefully be an inspiration for many.

Meet Dad

It's doubtful Dad set out to be a failure; although, he *did* seem to work hard at it once he became convinced that he was no good.

This man, my father, could play four or five instruments by ear. He was a great story teller. He could draw or paint captivating likenesses of family members, and not just of those he knew well. The pastel drawing he did in 1963 of Mrs. Kennedy's look of sorrow following President Kennedy's assassination makes the viewer feel the intensity of her pain. The First Lady had plenty to cry about. As it turned out, so did our family.

Dad gave in to his emotions. He also gave in to drink. It became the salve for his wounded spirit. Unpredictable by nature, he left our family dangling like a yo-yo, waiting to be yanked up and re-wound as taut as thread on a spool. Eventually, he'd let go and once again, we'd find ourselves dangling—until the next time.

As the youngest of four, I'd been spared the misery of Dad's most severe bouts of drinking. My brother and sisters had not. I must have been an adult, although I don't recall my age, when I first heard the story of how my dad came close to strangling my oldest sister, Patricia, during one of his binge-drinking episodes.

The story, as recounted to me by siblings, happened in February 1945, just as World War II was coming to an end. At the time, I was just six months old. Their descriptions were so vivid, I can visualize the scene.

* * * * *

It happened on a Sunday in February. My family, dressed in their finest clothes, had returned from attending Holy Trinity Anglican Church in our hometown of Welland, Ontario. Not my dad. He had little interest in the things of God. He repeatedly said, "My father, who went to church every Sunday and then sinned all week, was the biggest hypocrite around."

As the dinner hour approached, ten-year-old Shirley reached up into the cupboard and grabbed the dinner plates. She handed them to Trisha who was standing, hands on hips, tapping her foot on the frayed burgundy scatter rug in front of the kitchen sink.

Trisha took the five pink-and-white flowered china plates from Shirley's hands and laid them on the counter. Dora, our mother, continued to slice leftover potatoes to fry for Sunday's supper.

"I'm putting Claudia down in her crib while we eat," said Trisha. "She was out on the porch today, but I brought her in because of the cold. She cried the whole time she was out there." Trisha turned to leave the kitchen.

Mom kept her head down while she took the spatula and turned the potatoes over in the skillet. Her dull, dark hair, escaping from its bobby pins, hid her blue eyes.

Shirley's shoulders drooped. She glared through her horn-rimmed glasses at her disappearing sixteen-year-old sister.

"You mean you're leaving me to set the table all by myself, again?" she screeched.

Mom remained silent as she removed the pot roast from the oven.

"Stop that complaining in there and set the damn table!" Dad hollered from the living room.

Twelve-year-old Carl looked up from his library book. He stared at Dad lying on the couch. Our father seemed unaware of his presence—my quiet, pale brother with the brush cut sat awkwardly nearby on the threadbare upholstered chair. Carl muttered to himself as he slipped the stub of a movie ticket between the pages of his book. "No point in sitting here."

Book in hand, he tiptoed out of the room, past the kitchen, into his bedroom at the back of the house and quietly closed the door.

"Come for supper, now," called Mom a few minutes later.

As the family gathered in the dining room, Carl, dressed in his church clothes—white long-sleeved shirt and grey wool trousers—seated himself at the table to the right of Dad. Freckle-faced Shirley pulled out her chair and sat next to Mom, who was at the head of the table. Trisha, her long brown wavy hair sitting loosely around her shoulders, frowned as she looked at Dad and grimaced as she breathed in the air around her. She was left to sit the closest to Dad.

When all heads were bowed, Mom prayed aloud, "For what we are about to receive, we give thanks to you, Lord. Amen."

"Claudia's tucked into her crib, Mom," Trisha said. I fed her some pablum and gave her eight ounces of milk in her bottle."

Mom looked up, gave Trisha a half smile and nodded her head. She quietly cut the pot roast on the plate before her into small jagged slices.

"I'm going to look for a job in Buffalo next week, Dora," Dad said. "Carl Jones told me I could make some money as a paper-hanger there. He told me there are lots of jobs." The roar of his voice sliced through the silence. Mom said nothing and continued to cut the meat.

Trisha curled her upper lip as she turned and looked at Dad. She was still angry with him for riding her new two-wheel bike to the beer parlour on Friday. It had stayed there all night. Because Dad could hardly walk, let alone ride a bike, a friend had brought him home. Mom had chewed him out when he staggered through the door and hadn't spoken to him for the rest of the weekend.

"Hah!" taunted Trisha. "I just bet you're going to look for a job."

Dad's deep blue eyes narrowed as he grabbed his dinner plate. He picked it up and smashed it down on the table; then, jumping up from his teetering chair, he moved toward Trisha as she ran for the living room. A fiery blind rage swept over our tall, thin father. His black hair was dishevelled. His face contorted, communicating the ugliness of his fury. Dad charged toward Trisha. Mom, Carl and Shirley followed.

Trisha braced herself against the living room wall as Dad came at her, flailing his arms. As he raised both hands to Trisha's neck, Mom grabbed the shirt sleeve of his left arm.

"Stop it, Claude!" she said as she held out her other arm in an attempt to shield Carl and Shirley from his rage.

Dad abruptly swung down his arm and hit Mom in the stomach.

"Claude," Mom's eyes widened as she grabbed her abdomen, "you hit me!"

Carl began to cry while Trisha ducked down and around Mom and Dad in order to back out of the living room. She stood by the entrance staring at the scene before her.

Dad turned toward Mom. His eyes watered; his face sagged.

"I'm sorry, Dora, so sorry."

Mom turned away from him and walked toward the hallway. Shirley stood motionless. Two pools of tears surfaced as her bottom lip began to quiver. She turned her head and stared out of the front window overlooking the snow-covered porch. She sucked her breath in deeply and let out a sob.

Carl sniffed, closed his eyes and pressed his fingers against his eyelids. Dad collapsed onto the living room couch with his hands covering his face. Everyone was leaving while Dad sat alone.

"I'm going to the baby," said Trisha. She spun around and moved down the hallway. "She's crying."

Mom went into the hall closet and put on her black woollen coat. She tied a red scarf around her head, pulled on her rubber boots and went out and stood on the snow-covered porch. Ten minutes later, she walked back into the house. She removed her outer clothing, turned and walked briskly into the kitchen.

Our mother eased the dishrag from Shirley's hands so she could wash the pots and pans. Carl and Shirley stood silently beside her, glances darting back and forth between them.

Shirley took another tea towel from the drawer and began drying. The three worked in silence.

Later, Mom peered into the living room. Dad lay curled up on the couch. She shook her head, turned around and went into my room. "Don't ever ridicule your father again," Mom cautioned.

Trisha stared at her but said nothing.

A few weeks later, our mother had issued her ultimatum to Dad. If he didn't quit drinking, she would leave him.

For the next eleven years, with the help of Alcoholics Anonymous, Dad had remained sober. But, when I turned twelve years old, my life abruptly changed.

2

Life on 3-A Highway

Our family moved from Welland in 1949, when I turned five years of age. By then, Dad had been sober for four-and-a-half years. The two-storey house where we lived was located on the outskirts of the city. We lived on 3-A Highway for the next five years.

★ ★ ★ ★ ★

"You're going to get a lickin' when we get home," said Daddy.

Why does Daddy say lickin'? I lick an ice cream cone. It's not something done on a little kid's behind.

I looked up at Daddy as we drove home from visiting Mama's friend, Ivy. Daddy's hair was the colour of black treacle. It was all thick and wavy. His eyes were dark blue. People who knew Daddy and me said our eyes were the same colour. It always made me smile when I heard that.

I wasn't happy that my teeth were like Mama's with a big space between the two front ones. The gap was so wide that I could suck a soft spaghetti noodle right through the middle. I *did* like Mom's curly, black hair. Mine was dark brown and poker straight. I would have traded my teeth for Mama's hair.

I'm only seven years old and going into grade two. My teeth aren't fully grown yet. Maybe they'll grow together.

Even though Daddy said he would give me a "lickin'," it would be Mama who would take the fly swatter to the back of my legs—that's what usually happened when I got into trouble.

"Why did you keep on yakkin' when I told you I didn't want to stay after Ivy served her dessert?" Daddy asked Mama, as we sat crowded together in the cab of his pick-up truck. "Why?"

Mama stared straight ahead and didn't answer. She was still mad at me for telling Ivy that her tarts were stale.

"But, Mama, those tarts *were* stale," I wailed. "Am I supposed to say they tasted good when they didn't? You told me never to lie so how come I'm in trouble?

"You were being a rude little girl, Claudia, and I've told you about that too!"

In those days, Mama worked at the Darling Hat Shop in Welland, every day of the week except Wednesday afternoon and Sunday. I loved those afternoons when she was at home because she would make me one of my favourite suppers: shepherd's pie, spaghetti, macaroni and cheese or salmon loaf. On those afternoons, we didn't eat the leftover meat from that week's Sunday roast, but I could expect four-day-old slices of beef again on Thursday.

After Daddy picked Mama up from work on Wednesdays at noon, Mama would eat a cheese sandwich when they reached home. Then she'd fill a plastic tub with soapy water and get down on her hands and knees to scrub the floors with a bristly scrub brush. After the floors had dried, she would finish up by setting down the tub of wax beside her as she knelt on the floor. With a rag torn from a worn-out flannel bedsheet, she would shine up the floor until I could practically skate on it. Sometimes, we would go to Ivy's house when Mama had finished, but most often we went to my Grandma Philp's, because, most of all, Daddy liked visiting his mother.

When we arrived home from that visit with Ivy, I headed for the bathroom. *Wish we'd gone to see Grandma Philp this time.* Daddy picked up our long-haired, tortoiseshell cat—Fluffy—and stroked her back as he walked down the hallway to the kitchen.

"Get up on the toilet seat, Claudia. I'll be there in a minute," said Mama.

"Aw-w c'mon, Mama," I whimpered.

"Do as you're told!"

I stood on the cream-coloured toilet seat, faced the wall and waited. I looked at the chipped yellow paint next to the towel rack and then at the two faded green towels hanging from it.

Can't even dry myself with those towels; they're as scratchy as that wool blanket on top of my bed.

"Stand still, now," said Mama as she swatted the back of my legs with the first flick of the fly swatter. A second swat followed. When it was over, my legs burned like the bottom of a hot frying pan.

Mama left the bathroom while I continued to howl and rub the back of my legs. I jumped down from the toilet seat, grabbed the closest washcloth from its rung and turned on the tap until cool water poured from its spout. I put the cloth on the back of my leg while the water streamed down onto the red-and-beige tile floor. Then, I did the other leg—wailing all the while.

Ivy's tarts were stale. That's the truth. Don't know why I had to get the fly swatter for that!

"Stop that bawling in there or I'll give you something to cry about," yelled Daddy.

I never understood why Daddy said that. It hurt like crazy, and I did have something to cry about. Right now, he had the cat which adored Dad's frequent caresses, so I didn't even have the comfort that Fluffy often gave me. I continued to cry.

Even though Daddy said he would spank me, he hardly ever did. I only remember his spanking me once, when fat old Charlie Thompson stopped by for a visit. Charlie gave me a hug when he walked through our front door, and I stuck my tongue out at him. He smelled like a pile of dead wet leaves. Daddy let out a snort but when he told me he was going to give me a lickin', I crawled under the kitchen table. Daddy caught my arm and dragged me out but only gave me a light pat on my backside. It never even brought tears to my eyes.

My mother always did what she said she was going to do. As a child growing up in her household, I found her to be as regimented as a guard at Buckingham Palace. While on duty, she didn't smile, hug, move or do anything that didn't hold a purpose. Whenever she took the fly swatter to the back of my legs, she did so with steely resolve until she completed two whacks on the back of each leg.

Back then, I loved my father better. In my child's mind, he was the best dad ever.

* * * * *

1952

I could feel the weight of someone sitting on my bed as I rolled over. On the edge of it, sat my whisker-faced dad with dark circles under his eyes.

"Good morning, Daddy," I said as I squinted and pulled myself up to lean back on both elbows. I could see the sun filtering through the thin patterned cotton curtains that hung in the room I shared with Shirley and Patricia.

"I have a surprise for you—something that you have wanted for a long time," he said.

"Really? A two-wheeler? My birthday was in August, Daddy. Did you have to save up for it for another month?"

Daddy's stony look told me that I had guessed wrong.

"A baby brother—you have a baby brother," he said as his face broke into a wide grin.

I've never wanted a baby brother. Where did he get that idea? Why did he think that? A baby costs a lot more than a bike. If Mama and Daddy wanted to get me a baby, then at least they could have got a girl. What am I supposed to do with a boy? I don't even like boys.

My mother had hidden her pregnancy from everyone except my forty-seven-year-old father until her eighth month. She had kept this news from her older children until the bulk of her size necessitated full disclosure. I was the only one who was still unaware. Dad's announcement had definitely been a belated birthday surprise!

By the time Craig was born, on September 4, 1952, my sister, Patricia, was twenty four; my brother, Carl, twenty; Shirley, eighteen, and I was eight years old.

The month before, on August 8—my birthday—my mother had presented me with a gift-wrapped square box before she left for work. I plopped down on my bed and began twisting the bow's pink strands of ribbon around and around on my index finger.

"What's the matter?" my mother asked as she stood before me with her arms folded, "Why aren't you opening it?"

I looked up at her. She frowned.

Why does Mama wear that same dress every day? She looks fat in it.

I began taking off the wrapping paper.

Our family, 1945 (from left): Shirley, Mom, Patricia (Trisha), Carl and Dad holding me.

"Mickey Mouse puzzles!" I said trying to sound as pleased as I could. "I'll invite Janice over today. We can do them together. Thank you, Mama."

"Happy birthday," she said as she patted my head and walked swiftly out of my bedroom.

"I'm going to be late for work," I heard her mumble as she started down the stairs.

Puzzles aren't for summer. Bikes are for summer. I could ride a two-wheeler to Janice's house, and it would only take me five minutes instead of twenty. Why did I think I would be getting a bike? Yesterday, she told Daddy that she had to watch her pennies, now. Why?

After I got over my disappointment about getting a baby brother rather than a bicycle, I came to love Craig. In fact, I was pleased to have this round, angelic-faced, blue-eyed baby boy as a member of our family. His blond hair was like silk (except for the time he developed cradle-cap and Dad had to rub vegetable oil into the crusty scales on his head). As far as I could tell, he didn't cry much, just when he was hungry it seemed. Nobody ever complained about his crying so I considered him an easy baby to look after.

It had been necessary for my mother to go back to work soon after Craig was born. Daddy stayed home to take care of the baby, as well as looking after me when I came home from school and during the school holidays.

The year before Craig's birth, Shirley had moved to Toronto so she could find work. Hoping to change her profession from stenographer to that of a model, she had attended modeling school in the evenings. Her five-foot-eight-inch frame, slender body and attractive face gave her a good chance of success. After Craig's birth, Shirley gave up her dream and decided she had to come back home. She felt she was needed to help pay for the extra expense of Mom having another child to feed and clothe.

When my dad was able to work, Craig went to stay with Grandma Philp, Daddy's mother. By this time, Grandpa Philp, had demonstrated the complexity of a troubled man—troubled to the point where he had to be institutionalized. My Aunt Olive, who'd never married, lived with Grandma and helped her with Craig's care. Mom didn't breastfeed her baby; she didn't have the opportunity or the time. Feeding him a bottle made it easier for her to hand him over to someone else for tending. Maybe it wasn't easy for her, but she never talked about her innermost thoughts with her children. No one knew how Mom felt about anything, really— even how she felt about having a baby at the age of forty-four. Mom's pregnancy hadn't seemed to be a joyful time for her.

★ ★ ★ ★ ★

"Eyes on the board, Claudia," said Miss Casson.

I looked away from the classroom window and watched my grade three teacher as she stretched her long, thin arm toward the top of the blackboard to begin printing numbers for our arithmetic lesson. Her fingernails were painted a brilliant crimson. As I looked around the girl with the blond pigtails who sat in front of me, I could see Miss Casson's black wooden-heeled shoes. The seams of her nylon stockings were perfectly straight—right up to where her grey, woollen A-line skirt fell to the middle of her calves. A white, long-sleeved cotton blouse had been tucked into her waistband and her wide red cinch belt made Miss Casson appear even thinner than usual. When she smiled, her buckteeth poked out through her lips. I liked Miss Casson. She had the patience to teach a class of thirty-five eight year olds.

Even though I enjoyed attending Clarke Elementary School, I didn't like walking the mile and a half to and from school five days a week. Philip Logan took the same route. He had a freckled face and frowzy, dark brown hair. His furrowed brow seemed to be set for life by the age of eight; he was one mean kid and nobody liked him. The winter was the worst because when the snow was good for packing, he'd find stones along the side of the highway and stuff them in his snowballs. Then, he would throw them so hard that when they hit my thick, woolen snowpants, chunks of snow and stones would make their way down into the rubber galoshes that I wore over my shoes. Usually, by the time I got home, my shoes, socks and feet were wet. Often, I would walk on the other side of the ditch of 3-A Highway with my two friends, Janice and Dorothy, who lived nearby. When the three of us walked together, Philip didn't bother us much.

Most days, after school, when I walked up the steps of the back door that led to our kitchen, my dad would be inside either peeling potatoes or making other preparations for our supper. Often, Craig would be sleeping in his crib.

"Did that Logan kid bother you today?" Dad asked one afternoon when I returned home.

"Not today."

"I called the principal and told him he'd better do something about it," he said.

"You did? Thanks, Daddy."

I watched as he picked up my black boots from the scatter rug that lay inside the kitchen door. He wiped off the snow with a grey rag and set them down again.

"If he throws you in a snowbank or plows you with snowballs, again, I'll be calling his old man."

I could usually count on my dad to do things for me.

In one of the lower grades, I was selected to be a princess in the school play. I remember that I had to have a wand with a star on top. My dad said putting a few tiny stars on my dress would make the shiny flecks appear like the sequins on the dress of a princess.

Being creative and skilled with the ability to draw just about anything, Dad took a ruler and measured out seven different-sized stars on bristol board. Then, he cut them out and covered each one with silver foil, making sure they were smooth and shiny.

"What dress are you gonna wear for this thing you're in," Dad said as he finished pasting the last triangle of tinfoil on the front of each star.

I thought it was funny that he asked such a question because I only had one dress—the one I wore to church. But, Dad didn't go to church so he probably didn't notice.

"I'm wearing the light green dress with the little collar and puffy sleeves," I said.

"Go get it and I'll sew these stars on for you," Dad said as he finished up the last one.

I leaned my elbows on the kitchen table with my face held in my hands, watching. Dad selected a spool of light green thread from my mother's sewing basket. He put on his glasses, licked the end of the thread and pulled the thread through the eye of the needle. As he finished each star, he used a tool from his tool box to poke perfect holes near the points of each one. He turned my dress inside out and thrust the needle through the cloth and into the hole of the first star, all the while, carefully pushing the needle from the inside to the outside of the dress. He continued sewing until all of the stars were secured. Then, he rolled up another piece of bristol board, fastened it with tape and glued the largest star on top to make the wand.

"Here," he said as he handed me the dress and wand. "Go try on your dress and see how it looks."

Before taking the dress, I plunked down on his lap and gave him a hug that knocked his glasses to the middle of his nose.

"I'm going into the bedroom to look in your mirror." I grabbed both the dress and the wand as I slid off his lap.

I glided in my stocking feet down the hallway on our pine floors and went into Mom and Dad's bedroom. Off came my outer clothes and on went the dress. I looked at my image in the mirror on their dark walnut dresser. When I waved the wand, the little girl with the chubby face, dimpled cheeks and blue eyes grinned back.

After I had changed back into my light blue, short-sleeved tee-shirt and corduroy navy blue overalls, I returned to the kitchen.

"Well, do you like the way you look?" Dad said.

"It makes me feel like a *real* princess, Daddy."

"Well, that's what you are," he said. "Come sit on my lap while I draw you a picture of Mr. Jiggs,"

Mr. Jiggs, a cartoon character, had spiked hair, droopy eyes and a fat nose. Often, my dad would draw him with a cigarette hanging from his lower lip.

Dad used a black ball-point pen to draw each feature of Mr. Jiggs' head and rotund body. While he was drawing, Dad would tell me a story about him; something a child could relate to—something that might teach some kind of lesson.

There were so many things that I loved about my dad. Sometimes he would call out to me as he sat down at the piano in our living room. When he called my name, I would run to him and slide across the bench. Although the air around Dad often smelled of stale cigarette smoke, I would snuggle into his warmth.

Dad didn't have sheets of music on the piano ledge. Every song he knew, he had learned to play by ear.

Sometimes when we sat together at the piano, Dad would pound on the keys with all of the might of a carpenter hammering a nail into a board. I couldn't always understand the words to his songs, but I remember one song that he sang and played the most:

Show me the way to go home
I'm tired and I wanna' go to bed
Well, I had a little drink about an hour ago
And it went right to my head.
Wherever I may roam
On land or sea or foam
You can always hear me singing a song
Show me the way to go home. [1]

Another thing Daddy did that was fun, although kind of scary too, was when he'd invite me to sit on his shoulders. As he sat down, I would throw off my shoes and climb onto our dark brown couch and position myself behind him. Daddy would wait until I had put both legs over his shoulders before he stood up. First, he would wobble to one side of the room, bumping into the wall, and then he would wobble to the other side of the room and again— bump! I laughed my head off and tightened my arms around his neck. I knew he would never let me go. I knew I was safe, sitting high on his shoulders.

★ ★ ★ ★ ★

In 1953, Dad was admitted to the Toronto General Hospital for chronic back issues. It was in that year that he began to keep a scrapbook of letters from people. Later on, I would get to read them. Dr. Ian MacDonald, his surgeon, was someone my father had confided in. Dad engaged people in conversation and seemed to be liked by many. He also had a good sense of humour. Although Dad hadn't been educated past grade eight, he kept well informed. I recall many evenings after supper when he would park himself on the living room couch and read the *Welland Tribune* in its entirety.

★ ★ ★ ★ ★

1953

My mother was barely eking out a living to support our family of seven, but there we were, on June 2, 1953—Mom, Dad, Patricia and I—sitting in front of our new eight-inch, black-and-white television set. Arms folded and held tightly to her chest, my mother sat looking straight ahead; her mouth set in a firm line.

My dad had purchased our first television just before Elizabeth was officially crowned Queen of England. I remember that day as we sat in our living room waiting for Elizabeth to take her dramatic walk toward the throne.

How wonderful to be Queen Elizabeth! She will live in a beautiful palace with rooms as big as our little house. There will be television sets in every one, even in the bathroom. She'll have soft towels to dry herself with—as soft as a kitten's fur. She can have anything she wants. She'll never have to worry about having enough money for food and clothes.

Trisha and I gazed up at the set perched on top of our second-hand piano. Dad, as he took his seat beside my mother, looked down at her. She continued to scowl.

"Dora, I did this for you. You're from England, dammit! Can't I *ever* please you?"

At the time of Dad's purchase, Shirley, Carl and Trisha were all working and paying room and board. Dad worked sporadically. However, even with more money coming in, the extravagance of purchasing a television set had not been figured into Mom's budget.

"I'm going upstairs to get my camera," said Trisha. "For heaven's sake, everyone practise smiling!"

"C'mon, Dora, let's smile." Dad said to my mother, who was frozen on the other side of me. He slipped his arm behind my shoulder and drew me in close to him.

Mom continued to sit stiffly erect. I stared up at her. She looked wretchedly unhappy, sitting there in her faded mauve cotton house dress.

Trisha returned with her Kodak Brownie camera in hand and stood before us.

"Come on! Give me a smile everyone!"

"This will have to do, I guess," said Trisha as she pressed the shutter release.

She quickly placed the camera on the chair next to the piano and slumped down onto the couch on the other side of me.

The music began and the choirs started to sing. Mom unfolded her arms and looked up as the queen began her walk down the 300-foot aisle of Westminster Abbey for her coronation. Mom's face softened. She shifted her position on the couch and moved closer to me.

"I was born in England, you know, Claudia—Birmingham," said my mother.

"I know. And you know what, Mama? You look like Elizabeth's mother, especially when you smile with your mouth closed and you don't show that big space between your two front teeth. I like it when you smile, Mama. Even when I can see your teeth—I like it."

3

Back to Welland

1954

In the summer of 1954, the year I turned ten, our family moved to Welland. Daily life had become tough. Mom could no longer keep up the mortgage payments on our house on 3-A Highway. As Dad had to take care of Craig, he wasn't able to work even if a job had materialized for him. So, we moved into the back apartment of my Grandma Philp's house. It seemed to be the only affordable option.

An addition had been built onto the back of Grandma's house as living quarters for her daughter Dorothy, her son-in-law, Osborne, and their three children. When Aunt Dorothy and Uncle Osborne bought a house across the street from Grandma Philp, we moved into the vacant apartment. The timing couldn't have been better.

Changing from a two-storey house with three bedrooms, a living room, dining room and kitchen, into the confined space of a two-bedroom apartment with a kitchen, a living room and a closet-sized bathroom—only big enough for a toilet—made it necessary for my grandmother to give up one of her vacant upstairs bedrooms.

As Grandpa Philp had been institutionalized—"away"—since 1953, my mother, father and Craig had taken over the bedroom that had been his, and Carl had a room of his own. Trisha, Shirley and I shared the same room. They slept in a double bed. I slept in a single bed across from them.

We no longer had the comfort of Fluffy curling up on the beds. I was so allergic to him that I had become seriously ill. We had been forced to give our friend away. I think Dad and I missed him the most. Dad would have to wait until later to adopt Snowball, who lived to be seventeen years old.

It was irritating for my older sisters to have me sleeping little more than an arm's length away.

"Stop that whispering, Claudia. We have to get up for work in the morning!" either Trisha or Shirley would plead.

I'd stick my thumb in my mouth—for I still did that until the age of ten—and like a corked bottle floating in the sea, I would close my eyes and drift off.

★ ★ ★ ★ ★

After our family moved to Welland, I hung around the house for the first few weeks. However, one warm, sunny summer day a girl scuttled up the back steps that led to our apartment and knocked on our door.

"Hi! I'm Patsy, Patsy Buchanan, from up the street. Wanna' go 'cross town with me to the swimming pool?"

I smiled at the friendly girl with the short black curly hair and greenish-blue eyes.

I wonder if the freckles on her nose and cheeks bother her as much as Shirley's did when she was a kid. Shirley used to hate them!

Later, Patsy told me that her mother had said I needed a friend. Our mothers, having played in the same card club, had known one another for years.

Patsy and I became best friends fast! I liked that she smiled whenever she spoke. There was no other person I knew who laughed as much and as loudly as she did.

My new friend invited me to go everywhere with her: shivery swims in the Welland canal with her other friends, twenty-five cent movies at the musty Capitol Theatre in town and giggly sleepovers at her house.

I often felt homesick when I slept over at Patsy's house. Even though I loved being there, sleep didn't come quickly. When the lights were turned out, I tried stifling my tears by turning my face into the pillow. My soggy pillowcase made it even more difficult to sleep. It took hours! I would lie as motionless as Patsy's plastic doll, the one that sat in the corner of her room, legs sticking straight out of the miniature wooden highchair. I didn't want Patsy, who was sound asleep beside me, to know what a crybaby I was. *Who would want a crybaby as a friend?*

On these sleepovers, I frequently thought of my mother. Mrs. Buchanan didn't work outside of the home as Mom did. She stayed at home and took care of the family while Patsy's father went to work at one of the steel companies in Welland. When Mr. Buchanan came through the door at supper time, the way Mrs. Buchanan, Patsy and Billy, her younger brother, greeted him with a hug or a kiss warmed me all over. At the same time, it made me kind of sad because I had never seen my mom and dad exchange a kiss or a hug. Ever!

"How was everyone's day?" Mr. Buchanan would often ask.

Patsy and Billy would sometimes begin speaking at the same time.

"Okay, you first, Patsy," Mr. Buchanan would say holding up his hands. "Billy, ladies first, remember?" he would chide.

This family must be normal—not at all like mine.

Dad with Carl, circa 1936.

4

Carl

1954

Sounds of breaking glass crashed through the barrier of my deep sleep—my two sisters shrieked. Inside my ten-year-old mind, a burst of fear ignited terror. Footsteps thumped toward the room where my brother Carl slept. A clamour of frenzy followed. Shirley and Trisha pushed back their covers, scrambled out of bed and rushed toward the hallway. Craig's cries could be heard coming from Mom and Dad's bedroom.

Over and over again, my Dad shouted Carl's name. It wasn't the first time my brother had woken the family during one of the night's darkest hours.

Mom's calm voice gave orders. "Patricia, call Dr. Purdon. His number is by the phone. Shirley, pick Craig up, take him downstairs and warm up a bottle for him."

I remained frozen, gripping my blanket and flannel sheet under my chin. I put the sheet up to my nose to inhale the fresh smell of laundry detergent. As it reminded me of Mom, it gave me a moment's comfort. In an attempt to hold back distressed sobs, I shut my eyes tight. My stomach began to heave as I felt the dread of some unknown horror. Riveted with fear, I remained mute—afraid that any moment I would hear the bad news, "Carl's dead." Had he dived from his second-storey bedroom window and died from the fall? This time, had another nightmare actually killed him?

* * * * *

The first such occurrence had happened in the summer of my eighth year. The room that I shared with Shirley and Patricia had been as dark as a mudhole. There'd been no moon in the sky to cast light through the curtains of our second-storey window. Absent were the shadows that would cause me—a child with a heightened imagination—to tremble, while waiting for sleep to rescue me from my fears of the dark.

Each night, as my sisters crawled into their double bed, I felt sheltered and protected.

Sleep came quickly with Shirley and Trisha nearby. In part, I placed the blame for my fear of the dark on Carl. He delighted in chasing me into a closet and then telling me I was sharing space with the bogeyman! I didn't know Carl had nightmares, causing nocturnal wanderings, until the time he tumbled down the stairs that led from the hallway outside his bedroom.

On that summer night, I'd been awakened by a loud thud. It sounded like a bowling ball thundering down an alley, hitting the pins with a forceful shattering sound. I bolted upright.

"Carl," Trisha groaned.

Dazed, I fell back on my pillow.

My two sisters left the bedroom and stood at the top of the stairs. From my bed, I could see Shirley with her hand over her mouth, standing motionless, while Trisha zipped out of sight, down the stairs.

Mom and Dad, their bedroom on the main floor, were already tending to Carl. Although I could hear them speaking in muffled tones, I didn't know what had happened. It seemed like hours before Dad finally came upstairs to my room. What a relief it was to be assured that Carl was okay, although bruised and cut. Mom was bandaging his arm and hand.

My brother's night terrors puzzled me. For many months afterward, I feared it would happen again. No one spoke further to me about the incident, and I didn't ask questions. For some reason, our family seemed to deal with things as they occurred and then moved on. Possibly, that helped me not to dwell on the horror— until it happened again.

★ ★ ★ ★ ★

Now, once more thrown into a nightmare world, I squeezed my eyes shut. Maybe if they were tight I could crush the reality out of what had happened. I held my breath to keep from sobbing.

I mustn't cry. If I do, I'll most definitely throw up.

I was forgotten. Mom and Dad were outside with Dr. Purdon and Carl while Shirley and Trisha were carrying out Mom's orders. I felt abandoned and fearful that my brother had been killed during his latest nightmare. Alone with my thoughts, I faced the wall.

If Carl's dead, he won't have a wedding in August. He won't marry Bev, and she will be all alone. I love Carl and Bev. I don't want him to die. I want Bev as my other sister. She's good to me, inviting me out with her and Carl on their dates—especially to the beach. And I remember once when we went to the beach; Carl came out of the water and I told him he had big tits. Carl didn't laugh, but Bev did. That helped me feel a little better as my face went so hot. I stood and stared at the sand.

To me, Bev always looked beautiful whether she was smiling or not. She had Lucille Ball lips—curvy and full. Her dark brown eyes sparkled when she laughed, like there were tiny candles sitting inside of her pupils.

I gulped and began to whimper.

"Mom! Mom!" I shouted.

Silence.

Footsteps were coming up the stairs.

"Daddy, what happened to Carl?"

Dad stood beside my bed. "He's gonna' be okay. He had a nightmare and crashed through his window. Doc Purdon said the clothesline saved him—broke his fall. Go back to sleep," he said and then touched me on the top of my head with his hand.

Go back to sleep?

As Dad turned and walked toward the door, I began to shake.

"Where are you going? Don't go. *Please.*"

"I'm goin' back to bed. I'm beat."

"Don't close the door, Daddy!"

He left it open, said goodnight and left.

Sleep wouldn't come. I waited for Shirley and Trisha to come back to bed. I heard the slow movement of feet ascending the stairs. After Shirley had put Craig down in his crib, she entered our room behind Trisha.

"I'm scared."

"Go to sleep, Claudia," said Shirley. "Mom's with Carl. They'll be up in a minute." *What if Carl goes back to bed and has another nightmare, maybe even dying this time?*

"But what if...."

"Never mind thinking about it. Go to sleep, now," said Trisha.

How can I sleep? I'm going to have nightmares. Carl's supposed to get married in two weeks. Will he crash through the window again? Nobody talks to me about anything.

Once more, I rolled over to face the wall. I did the one thing I knew would bring me enough comfort to fall asleep. My thumb had been tucked under the fingers of my right hand. I brought it out of its warm cocoon and thrust it into my mouth. I began to suck like a hungry baby latched onto her mother's breast.

* * * * *

Carl married Bev on August 28, 1954. Following that latest nightmare, he had begun to receive psychological counselling. There were no more violent incidents. Eventually, the nightmares stopped. No one ever spoke about Carl's sleepwalking nor did we know the root cause of them. Our speculation was that it had something to do with Dad's behaviour.

* * * * *

Trisha's wedding had been set for November later the same year. However, her marriage to Bill Watt, a military man, had to be moved to the middle of September, due to the fact that he had been posted to Kentville, Nova Scotia. He was required to report for duty by the first of September. Trisha, with Bill's father, flew out, but no one in our family could afford a plane ticket. The rest of the Watt family had other commitments.

How I sobbed about the loss of my sister who, over the years, had become like a second mother to me. Trisha was the one who had showered me with hugs and kisses. On nights when Mom wasn't at home, Trisha would tuck me in, say my prayers with me and plant a kiss on my cheek before she left the bedroom.

While I missed Shirley living at home when she married Bob Mason in 1956, it was Trisha's move to Nova Scotia that left me feeling pangs of sorrow.

* * * * *

At our house, Dad continued to make dinner most weeknights. Our small kitchen often reeked of the corn oil he used frying left-over boiled potatoes.

"Dad, you forgot to turn the gas down! The oil is burning! The kitchen is smoky. Where *are* you?" I screeched as I hurried down from my bedroom, one winter afternoon.

"I'm in the can!" he hollered from the hallway bathroom that separated Grandma's kitchen from ours.

"Turn off the gas and open the back door," he yelled. "I'm pukin'!"

I did what I was told.

Why is Dad suddenly so sick? He seemed fine when I came home from school this afternoon. What's going on?

* * * * *

By late 1955, Dad was working sporadically as a house painter. On those days, Craig went to a nursery that was run by Roman Catholic nuns. After work, Dad would pick up Craig, and often they would visit with Grandma Philp until it was time to fetch Mom. When Mom got home at 6:30 p.m., she would serve the supper Dad had prepared beforehand.

Throughout the meal, three-year-old Craig would chatter and our forks and knives could be heard scraping across the plates. Apart from that—silence.

Sometimes, I would notice my mother scowling at Dad and shaking her head scornfully, even though he hadn't said anything. For some reason, I knew enough to keep my mouth shut.

Why does she seem annoyed with Dad? He hasn't said or done any-thing that I can see.

Dad never seemed to catch Mom's scornful head shaking. She

always did it while his eyes were cast down or when he went into the living room after he finished his meal.

I don't understand.

Since we had moved to Welland, there was something different about Dad. He had an unfamiliar odour. His smell kind of reminded me of rotting fruit.

Maybe Mom doesn't like that smell either.

5

Trisha

1955

Mom and Dad sat side by side on the living room couch as they watched *The Ed Sullivan Show*[2] on our twelve-inch television set. Not me. I sat next to the table on one of the grey-mottled vinyl chairs in our kitchen—waiting. I wanted to be the first one to fling my arms around Trisha when she walked through our back door. It was Sunday night. She and Bill were already a half-hour late.

"It's going to be a re-ally, re-ally, big sh-o-o, tonight folks," said Mr. Toast-of-the-Town.

Hah, he says that every week. Get a new line, Mr. Sullivan!

I looked down at the silver handmade ring on my middle finger. It was too big for me, but Dad had wrapped a thin strip of masking tape inside the ring to make it fit better. Trisha had bought it from her friend who designed and made jewellery in Kentville, Nova Scotia. A Viking ship, also made of silver, had been mounted on the top of the ring.

Trisha gave this to me for Christmas, just last week. It's the day after New Year's and she's already leaving…again.

The sound of a man's footsteps on the snow-packed steps became louder. The door opened. I shivered. Was it the icy night air or the excitement of the moment?

"Hi, kiddo," Bill said as he backed up against the open door. I looked up at him and grinned. Flakes of snow covered his blond eyelashes. Beads of moisture had settled on his hairline. Bill must have been about 6'1" and was, for sure, good-looking. He had vibrant blue eyes and a smile that curved upward like a half moon.

As Trisha walked through the doorway, she began stamping her feet. Snow fell on the maroon and beige scatter rug beneath her brown galoshes. Her close-cropped hair had white crystals crowning her head. She was dressed in the full-length muskrat coat that Bill had given her as a Christmas gift. After Trisha removed her boots, she opened her arms to me. I burrowed my face into the shoulder of her coat.

"You're late and you're leaving tomorrow." I moaned.

"But, we'll be back next summer. It won't be a year from now like it was this time."

Her comment brought little comfort to me.

I lowered my head. I made a fist with my fingers against my leg, and began counting off the months until July.

My mother came into the kitchen as Bill began to help Trisha with her coat. He leaned over and gave Mom a kiss on the cheek.

"Hello, Mom," he said.

"Hello there, you two!"

Bill handed my mother Trisha's coat. Mom ran her right hand down the fur sleeve, smoothing down its nap. Then, she folded the coat over her arm and walked into the living room.

First, Mom opened the door of the living room closet under the stairs and hung the coat on a wire clothes hanger. Mom stood searching. She removed the camel hair coat that had once belonged to my grandfather, and put Trisha's coat on the only wooden hanger in the closet. After laying grandpa's coat on the floor, she closed the closet door.

Dad continued to watch television as Bill went into the living room. Bill walked over and greeted him with a handshake. Dad smiled up at Trisha, while Mom switched off the set when Bill and Trisha sat down next to Dad.

"Claudia, go tell Grandma and Aunt Olive that Patricia and Bill are here," said Mom. "They'll want to say 'good-bye.'"

"Okay," I said as I began climbing the stairs.

"Wait—why aren't you going through the kitchen?" Mom asked.

I took the stairs two at a time and didn't answer my mother.

When I entered my bedroom, I opened the dresser drawer. On top of my nylon slip, in a plastic bag, lay Trisha's wedding corsage. I pulled it out of the packet and cupped it in the palm of my hand while I examined the artificial white carnations. Her corsage was trimmed in pink satin ribbon which was covered with silver glitter. I brought it up to my cheek—then to my nose—I inhaled the fading fragrance of Trisha's perfume. I stuck my hand back into the bag and pulled out her note: "Dear Claudia: This is the only 'bouquet' I had. I wore it on my dress. Love, Patricia."

After I read her note, I folded it up and tucked it back under the corsage in the plastic bag. When the precious sachet was again nestled in the closet drawer, I darted out of my bedroom, through Mom and Dad's room and into Grandma Philp's part of house. All the while, I twisted my silver ring around my middle finger.

Six more months until Trisha comes back. What will I do with my sadness? Christmas is over, school starts tomorrow and she'll be gone!

Mom before leaving for work in the late fifties.

6

My mother and me

I'm not sure when it occurred to me how hard my mother worked, but when it did, I began to feel differently toward her. I no longer viewed her as a cold, punitive parent. I remember lying on my bed one night, working myself up into a good cry: *What will I do if anything happens to Mom?*

★ ★ ★ ★ ★

"Claudie, will you comb my hair for me when I come upstairs after I finish doing the laundry?" Mom stood wiping her hands on her orange-and-white checked apron.

I watched as she stuck out her lower lip and then blew upward at the black curl that had fallen over her left eye. Each fine strand descended gently back onto her forehead.

Whenever Mom used the nickname she had given me, I nearly swooned. Mom didn't often use words in an endearing way, but when she did I believe it was a feel-good moment for both of us.

"Uh-huh. I'll rub your head and fix a new hairdo for you, too!"

I pictured my mother leaning back on her chair with me standing behind her making lines on her scalp with the point of her comb. I'd lift each lock of her hair, wind it around my finger to make a tight curl. No bobby pin needed! Each curl would stay in place like a well-trained child who had been told, "Sit still. Don't move!"

Mom looked at me, opened her mouth slightly, clenched her teeth and made a clicking sound of approval. It made me think of Fred Astaire when he would tap his shoe back and forth.

I wish I could take tap dancing lessons again. I liked being on stage. Everybody in the family came to see me. They told me that I looked pretty in my green-and-orange costume with the little fish stuck on my skirt. I wish Mom could afford to send me back for lessons again. It was only one dollar a week.

I handed Mom the green-and-white china tea cup and saucer. She tipped the cup up to her chapped lips and sipped the hot, steaming liquid. She peered at me over the cup's rim.

"Tea has to be good and hot to be enjoyed," she said.

★ ★ ★ ★ ★

The cellar gave me the creeps. It was damp with an overpowering musty smell. The ceiling beams were low, and cobwebs had settled on the wooden joists in each corner. On the cord where the light-bulb dangled over the sink, a spider, the size of a nickel, crawled toward the light. Shuddering, I feared a prehistoric beast, like in *Creature from the Black Lagoon,*[3] would rise up from the drain, scoop me up and take me away to a place of torture.

I backed away from the drain and headed toward the stairs. I waited there for Mom to drink her tea. She turned away from the laundry tubs and sat down on one of my grandmother's wooden chairs, the chair that had only one spindle missing. She crossed her legs as she leaned back and sipped the hot liquid. I guessed the tea gave her the extra burst of energy she would need to finish the tedious job of doing laundry in a wringer washer.

Mom *had* to be tired. Every day she got up at 5:30 a.m. and laboured non-stop. She even worked as she came down the stairs each morning. With a dust rag in hand, she would wipe each of the pine steps as she crept backward to the bottom. No dustball was left behind.

While Dad prepared most of the meals and drove Mom to and from work, the demands of earning an income outside the home and running the household fell to Mom, and she had little time or energy for anything else.

My mother did most things single-handedly. Each day of the week had its household task, which she began after she washed the supper dishes. A woman with exceptional energy and unfailing dedication to her family and to God, she weathered all hardships. Mom demonstrated the type of endurance, discipline and strength of a rock climber determined to reach the summit.

As Mom handed me back her empty cup I asked, "Will you be coming up in time to watch *I Love Lucy?*"

My mother rarely saw her favourite show in its entirety. Once she had slumped down in her soft cushioned chair in the living room, put on her pink knitted slippers and placed her feet up on the red vinyl hassock, she would often begin snoring within ten minutes. Her snores were short, soft purring sounds coming from the middle of her throat.

I could see that Mom still had towels to wash, rinse and put through the wringer. Tonight she would be hanging the laundry on the basement clothesline used during winter months.

"I'll try," she said as she looked at the washing lying on the side of the porcelain sink, "I'm making good time."

I'm glad tomorrow is Tuesday. At least she'll be in the kitchen while she irons. I'll have her close by, then.

I walked back upstairs and through my grandmother's kitchen. I crossed the linoleum floor and opened the door to the hallway that separated Grandma's kitchen from ours. The door to our apartment was slightly ajar. I leaned on it with my shoulder, backed into the kitchen with the cup and saucer in my hands and put them in the sink. As I went into the living room, I saw Dad lying on the sofa with his eyes closed.

"Dad," I whispered, not sure if I should wake him, "can I change the channel?"

He opened one eye, looked at me and turned over on his right side to face the back of the chesterfield. I sat down on the pink brushed-nylon chair next to the couch. I didn't touch the knobs on the television set. I began to watch the news.

A man was saying that on the first of December, 1955, Rosa Parks, a black woman, had just been arrested for refusing to give up her seat to a white passenger in Montgomery, Alabama.

What's wrong with people? Aren't all men created equal? Where did

I hear that? She has black skin. That doesn't mean that she's a bad person—that she should be arrested.

"Dad, I said softly, are you awake? I need to ask you something. Dad?"

My father rolled over and grunted but didn't answer.

7

Shame

1957

It was a Saturday afternoon in May. My two friends and I were
walking down the street feeling the fullness of spring sharing its
glorious summer promises. A cool breeze brought the sweet scent
of lilacs.

The three of us were enjoying a day free of the adolescent-
smothering routine of school.

"I want to stop by my house and show you my new outfit before
we go to the movies," said Jackie, as she nudged Patsy with her
shoulder. "We have time."

I looked at Jackie with her freshly permed hair. Her mom could
afford to send her to a hairdresser. So could Patsy's. My perms,
slaved over by my long-suffering sister, Shirley, came from a box
that contained plastic curlers and a solution that made our eyes
water until the last of the bitter-smelling stuff had been rinsed out
and had swirled down the drain.

Jackie's comment started me thinking about the new skirt that
my mother had promised me. *At last, something that isn't a hand-
me-down. I can hardly wait!*

"My mother—she's ordering me one of those pencil skirts from
the Sears' catalogue." I turned around to walk backward, facing
Jackie and Patsy.

"Oh, sure," Jackie sneered, "I just bet she is!"

Patsy winced as she lowered her head.

I guess I'm supposed to be ashamed 'cause I come from a family with so little money for new clothes.

I never knew what shame was until Jackie made fun of me that day. It made me feel as though I was different—that somehow, I wasn't the same as her and Patsy—that I was a liar and poor.

Jackie is looking down on me. She's not my friend; she's Patsy's. My chest tightened. It felt as though a big, black crow had been tearing away at my soul.

★ ★ ★ ★ ★

Fall 1957, brought its own devastating shock.

"You're in for a treat, teenyboppers," said the disc jockey. "Here's Gene Vincent singing 'Be-Bop-a Lula'!"[4]

W-e-ll—be-bop-a-lula, she's my baby...

I jumped out of bed, turned up the radio, hopped over my pile of *Little Lulu* and *Archie* comic books, and began to jive. I sang along with Gene. I knew all the words to most songs on the *Hit Parade*.

Ever since my mother had surprised me with a radio of my own, I would listen to it every day. Mom knew how much I loved music. She would have saved for at least six months to buy that radio.

My mother always planned well ahead for every anticipated expense. She would even write 'date of purchase' on the Kleenex boxes: the entire date, with month and year included. Then, she would stick it on the top of the box with masking tape. "I need to keep track of expenses," she would say. Mom stored her larger boxes of tissue in a kitchen cupboard, just in case she needed more for someone's cold. My mother was a practical and thrifty woman. Because of her efficiency, the family never ran out of toilet paper or Kleenex. Also, as soon as Christmas was over, Mom would start saving to buy presents for the following year.

Outside my bedroom window, raindrops made small puddles in our rutted gravel driveway. Thick dark clouds covered the sky to the left of my window, beyond the maple tree that blocked my view of the laneway, behind my grandmother's property. What a miserable day!

Even though the morning was gloomy and Mom had to work, I looked forward to the afternoon—I would be at rehearsal for the Welland Little Theatre's production of *Snow White and the Seven Dwarfs*. Patsy would be dropping by my house at 1:00 p.m. We always went together to the nearby high school for practice.

I loved being on stage with the other kids—singing, dancing. I would get lost in my role as one of the six yellow birds. Whenever Snow White was on stage, I would be by her side. It didn't cost Mom anything for me to be in the operetta. If it had, I wouldn't have been having any fun on Saturdays.

I turned the radio off and glanced at my Timex.

It's noon. Time to get dressed and eat—fast! What will I wear? Pants? Two choices: brown corduroy or navy blue. Navy blue. They'll look better with the long-sleeved, red cotton pullover Mom just washed and ironed. Warm cardigan? The cream-coloured one—thin at the elbows; at least it has every button.

After getting dressed, I went down to the living room. I approached my dad as he lay on the couch with his eyes closed. His thick, black moustache was matted. Dark whiskers with flecks of white covered his cheeks and chin. He didn't look like himself. He had never smelled so bad. A grey-painted milk bottle stood upright on the floor. My stomach turned sour at the smell of urine. As I stared at him, I remembered how his whiskers had burned my face when he used to brush his three-day growth of beard over my cheek.

"How do you like my whisker rub?" he would ask, like a proud gardener gliding the soft petal of a prize-winning rose across my cheek.

Although his whisker rub had felt like sandpaper that brought heat to my face, I still wanted his closeness. I often laughed when he did it a second time.

"Hi, Daddy," I said now. I looked at the red stains on his blue, black and white flannel shirt. Then, my eyes moved down toward his legs. A grey, woollen army blanket covered part of his lower body leaving one leg exposed—a skinny, white, hairless limb.

No response.

A glass of Ovaltine and a ham sandwich wrapped in waxed paper had been prepared by Mom for me to eat. Mom insisted that I, at least, take a nutritional drink in the morning. The Oval-tine—tasting like a mild dose of Kaopectate with a touch of choc-olate—made me gag if I drank it too fast.

I gulped down the last of the Ovaltine and gobbled up my sand-wich. Finished! I opened the door to the hallway where I would wait for Patsy. As I slipped my arms into my coat, Aunt Olive shuffled into the hall from Grandma's kitchen.

"Hi, Aunt Olive."

"Hello, dear. Are you going *tumwhere* today?"

Aunt Olive had been born with a severe hearing defect. When she spoke, she had difficulty pronouncing many of her words. For instance, she pronounced turkey as *kurkey*, and Sister Syder, her friend from church, as *Titter Tyder*.

Aunt Olive loved her ten nieces and nephews and spoiled all of us equally, with candy and little trinkets purchased with the allow-ance she received from my grandmother. We would often get our own way with her, but when she was cross with either one of her two brothers or her sister, she would become silent and moody. Sometimes she would strike back at them in some vindictive way. Today, my father was the target of her anger.

"Yup," I said to her question. "I'm waiting for Patsy. We're going to rehearsal together at Welland High School."

Aunt Olive stood facing me with her arms folded and held tightly to her chest. I looked at her expanding waist.

Look at that tummy! It's a party place, where all of the cookies and sweets she eats gather to cheer for each new pastry's arrival.

She walked into our apartment. Soon, she walked back out again.

"I see yer Dad is still restin' on the couch," she said. "He hasn't poken to me tince I came and got Traig before your mother went to work."

Her eyes narrowed.

"Yer Dad is a no good *ac-o-holic!* He's a *trunk*. He *tinks* because he been *trinking* all night!"

What is she saying to me? That horrid Ovaltine is coming up into my throat. Daddy is good. He's not a bad man. My heart is jumping around in my chest. I feel so hot. I can't breathe. Why is she saying these things? He didn't answer me when I said, "Hi." Doesn't he love me anymore?

*Grandpa Philp, Aunt Olive and Grandma Philp in Muskoka,
year unknown.*

*Dad, aged fifteen, on his 1919
Harley Davidson in 1923.*

I gulped and swallowed. Aunt Olive turned around and slammed Grandma's kitchen door behind her. I stood for a few minutes, breathing in rapidly and exhaling with deep sighs. I couldn't move.

After about five minutes, I heard a knock on the side door. Slowly, I opened it. "C'mon, Claudia, we're going to be late!" said Patsy. She spun around on the landing. Two-at-a-time, she took the steps toward our sidewalk.

I couldn't skip. I said nothing as I tried, with a fast-paced walk, to keep up to her. Tears spilled down my cheeks. I wiped them away with my coat sleeve. Fear and shame grabbed my throat.

What does it mean to have a drunk for a father? Snow White will be waiting for me. I have to be ready to dance and sing. I can't dance. I can't sing. I should have been cast as one of the Seven Dwarfs— Dopey—that's who. How come I didn't know?

The afternoon was cool, but the rain had stopped. Puddles had formed in the dips of the sidewalk. I started running through them, paying little attention to the dirty water splashing my pants and my beige wool coat. I wanted to go in the biggest puddle I could find, jump up and down and holler, "It's a lie!"

When Patsy reached the middle of the high school steps, she turned around and stared.

"Claudia—hurry up! Hey, look at your pants and coat. You're a mess! Why didn't you skip over the puddles like me?"

Patsy didn't wait for an answer. She ran up the rest of the stairs toward another girl she knew. I stumbled up the steps, alone.

Fear

1957

> *It stalked me as I walked toward*
> *The unfamiliar scene*
> *Grabbed and twisted all my thoughts*
> *Whatever could this mean?*
> *Its face was hidden oh so well*
> *Was covered by a shroud*
> *And as the veil was lifted*
> *Fear spoke to me out loud.*
> —Claudia Philp

Dad was an alcoholic! For the next seven years, I would live under his roof in a state of apprehension. A weekend bender would be as unpredictable as my recurring nightmares. They also turned a peaceful night's sleep into a battleground of relentless anxiety. Often, the same dream haunted me: a gang of boys—out to grab and torture me—chased me. Just as they almost reached me, I'd sit bolt upright, awake. My hand would grope for the lamp on the green plastic covered crate that was my bedside table. The light remained on until I stopped shaking. If I stayed awake long enough, the bad dream was unlikely to return. One nocturnal disturbance was more than enough.

★ ★ ★ ★ ★

While Mom had continued to work, Dad continued to stay at home to take care of Craig and me. Often, he made his potato fritters, with fried pork chops or chicken, for our supper. Dad seemed to enjoy cooking.

When he made his fritters, he would peel and slice two or three large potatoes, each slice, a quarter inch thick. All the while, the oil would be gurgling on top of our gas stove. Then, he'd mix flour, baking powder and water to make the batter. The batter would be just thick enough to coat the potatoes. Dad would whisk the ingredients until every clump of flour disappeared.

"That's the secret to making perfect fritters," he'd say.

After the slices of potato were coated, Dad would dip them into the oil. He used tongs to lower each one into the pot. My Dad was as methodical as a trained chef. He would deep fry them— only removing them from the pot when they would become the colour of a gold nugget.

The fritters made me feel kind of sick if I ate too many. Dad would always decide how many I should eat. I was expected to finish everything he put on my plate. It wasn't worth listening to him crab and complain if I didn't rave about his fritters.

"Well," he'd begin, "why the hell did I bother making so many if you don't like them?"

"I like them, Dad, but I am just too full to eat anymore."

Sometimes, he would look at me and shake his head. His displays of unreasonable contempt for me continued to gnaw away at our relationship. I eventually grew to detest my father. His unpredictable binge drinking was a major factor.

★ ★ ★ ★ ★

It was a Friday evening in June 1957. The lush maple tree in our backyard cracked like a whip as its branches hit against our living room window. An unexpected downpour was coaxing a storm to let loose in torrents of pent-up fury.

For the longest time, I sat on the rose-coloured chair beside the couch. *Where is Dad?* He had left for the local convenience store after he put Craig to bed earlier in the evening.

"I'm just going to pick up a pack of Black Cat cigarettes. Be back soon."

Did he go to the Rex Hotel, too?

I looked down at my watch.

I hope he picks up Mom. Please, God, don't let him come home drunk!

The last time my father was drunk was less than a month ago. I remembered how he looked. His eyebrows were crushed tightly against eyelids; his lips were drawn over his two decayed, yellow front teeth. Small beads of perspiration clung to his oily forehead.

Dad had picked up a dining room chair and lifted it high above his head. When he crashed the chair onto the living room rug, its oak back cracked and broke away from the seat. He stood still for a moment. My tears soaked my mother's flowered cotton dress as I turned my face into her thumping chest. She remained silent— one arm hung limp by her side. Dad charged out the kitchen door. *Slam!* Soon, the choking roar of a car engine tore the night as he sped away.

I have no recollection of what angered him that evening. The one thing I do remember was that he had been drinking. I never saw him actually drink; I had only smelled the overpowering stench of alcohol. It had become a familiar odour.

* * * * *

Now, another living nightmare! The kitchen door opened—the one that led to the hallway between our place and Grandma Philp's. I could hear Grandma walk across our linoleum floor in her thick-heeled clunky shoes. She glanced at me through the door of living room. Without speaking a word, Grandma turned back into the kitchen. She moved toward the door that led to our backyard and the adjacent driveway.

Grandma was attired in her usual daily garb consisting of a long-sleeved grey, light flannel ankle-length dress. She had a bib-like piece over the front and back of her dress. The bib had been sewn into a band that went around her thick middle. On her grey head, she wore a white net covering with a piece of ribbon attached to each side of the bonnet. The half-inch white ribbon fell loosely around her neck. This was the traditional outerwear of the women who attended the same church as Grandma—the Brethren in Christ church.

I had never seen her wear much that was different. She kept her dress on all day; right up until she put on her nightgown before bedtime. Grandma always wore thick, black stockings—winter, spring, summer and fall. Not once, had I ever seen the white of her legs.

Grandma was a devout woman who took her faith seriously. All matters of concern were given over to the Lord in prayer. I imagined my Dad, with his bouts of drinking, kept the knees of her stockings thinner than tissue paper.

As Grandma reached for the back door, she opened it. I could hear the rain cutting through the night air. A wind had picked up. Rain moved across the railing that led down to the plank at the bottom of the back steps. The wooden plank, which served as a sidewalk, ended beside the driveway.

"Claude," shouted Grandma, "don't start that—leave Dora alone!"

Is he hitting Mom? Is he pushing her?

Grandma stepped on the landing and walked out into the rain.

My stomach heaved. It felt just like it had last summer when I was at the highest peak of the rollercoaster as it made its rapid descent. I turned to climb the staircase from our living room. At that moment, Grandma came back into the house.

"Get upstairs and stay with Craig until your mother comes up," said Grandma.

Craig, who had been asleep on his cot, began to cry. A light-headed feeling came over me as I walked into his room.

"I want Mama," Craig pleaded.

He slid down from his cot and headed for the door.

"No—not right now," I said as I grabbed his hand.

I walked with Craig toward the doorway that led into Mom and Dad's room. Another door in their room led to the hallway where the upstairs bathroom was located. With my grip firm on Craig's hand, we entered the bathroom. *The key will be in the door. I can lock it.*

Craig looked up at me and began to cry again.

"I want Mama."

"Shush! She'll be up in a minute. You're a good boy. Don't worry. Mama will be here soon. She'll take you back to bed."

With Craig's hand in mine, we slid down the wall opposite the toilet, landing softly on the cold bathroom floor. My icy body shuddered even though the bathroom air was stuffy. A faint smell of urine took my breath away. *Yuck—Dad missed the toilet, again.*

Craig sat on my lap as I shifted my body toward the wash basin. Somehow, the fragrant smell of the Woodbury's hand soap, resting in the recess of the white porcelain sink, took the edge off my fear. It comforted me.

I thought about the bath that I took every Saturday morning in that claw-footed porcelain bathtub. The tub sat by the window that overlooked Grandma's white wooden arbour with its climbing plants.

The cold surface of the tub would soon warm up while I'd take my washcloth and soak it in the water. The steam would rise all around me. After I'd squeezed out the cloth, folded it and placed it behind my head, I would close my eyes as the water soothed me. The tap would continue to run until I had depleted the hot water tank of all the comfort it had to offer. I often stayed put until someone hollered at me to get out because they had to use the toilet.

My Saturday baths would sometimes lull me into a make-believe world where it was Christmas every day: our family sitting around the table, my Dad carving the turkey and everyone happy. That was the one day of the year I enjoyed most. Dad never drank on Christmas Day. We seemed like a normal family. There would be no yelling or arguments between Mom and Dad, no slamming of doors, no cursing. Peace without fear—on Christmas Day.

"You're a good boy, Craig," I repeated.

He stopped crying and looked up at me.

You're such a cute little guy with those wide-set blue eyes.

Craig leaned his damp blond head into my chest.

I heard the soft familiar sliding of my mother's slippers as she came toward the bathroom door. Finally!

"C'mon out," Mom said. "Patricia is here, Claudia. She's going to take you home with her for the night."

Craig and I stood side by side while I turned the key to unlock the door.

"Mama!" he cried.

My mother lifted Craig into her arms. Even with the baby of the family, Mom didn't show excessive affection. I looked up at her—waiting, hoping—but nothing. Deep furrows of worry ran in three straight lines across her forehead, lines that seemed to penetrate more deeply with the passing of time.

After Mom put Craig to bed, we walked down the stairs and into the living room. Dad was nowhere to be seen.

"Where's Dad?" I asked.

"He's gone with Grandma over to her part of the house. He's staying there for a while."

Mom walked with me to the side door of our apartment. Trisha, who had come back to Welland a few months before with her two children, Jamie and Robin, was waiting for me. We hugged.

Bill had been posted to a place in Southeast Asia and would remain there for one year. How overjoyed I was when I found out Trisha would be living close by.

"I'll keep Claudia with me tomorrow," said Trisha. "Will Craig stay with Aunt Olive?" she asked.

"Aunt Olive and Grandma will take care of him while I'm at work."

"Okay, I'll call you tomorrow."

Mom reassured Trisha that Dad was asleep and she would be fine. I followed Trisha down the steps toward her car.

"Good-bye, Mom," I said as I turned around to wave at her. My mother had already closed the door. Trisha and I walked to her car in silence. I had learned not to ask questions when my Dad's drunken episodes occurred.

"We don't talk about Dad," seemed to be the unsung mantra.

As we drove across town to Trisha's apartment, we shared little conversation. When we arrived, Trisha set up my bed on her living room sofa, putting down sheets, a pillow and blanket for me.

"See you in the morning, Claudia," said Trisha as she placed a glass of water on the end table by the sofa. "Jamie and Robin will be up early, so I hope you have a good night's sleep."

Trisha kissed my forehead. Then, she walked into her bedroom down the hall.

My feet are sticking over the sofa—they're cold. I can't sleep. What if I have a nightmare? I don't care if I always have to sleep on this couch.

I never want to go home, again.

Early in the morning, I heard my eighteen-month-old niece babbling in her crib. Robin would be so excited to see me.

Just then, Jamie walked into the living room.

"Wadda-you dooding here?" he asked in his three-year-old way.

"Just thought I would stay overnight so that I could spend the day with you and Robin."

"Go home!" he said as he walked over to turn the knob on the television set. Bugs Bunny appeared with carrot in hand. Jamie sat down in front of the screen. He folded his legs, one under the other. He set a bowl of dry Sugar Pops on the rug in front of him and began to eat them by the overflowing fistful.

I struggled up from the sofa and tiptoed from the living room into Trisha's bedroom. I slid under the covers with her. Her open eyes looked at me.

"Jamie doesn't like me. He told me to go home," I said, feeling the pangs of rejection.

"Is that so?" Trisha said as she moved closer to me. She placed her left hand gently around my neck. *Her touch—it feels good.*

"C'mon. What would you like me to make you for breakfast? I have some bacon. How about a toasted bacon and tomato sandwich?"

I really don't want to eat anything.

"Okay."

Weary from my fitful night's sleep, I was feeling almost sick to my stomach, yet, I wanted to please Trisha. She was generous with her love and hugs. Even though we hadn't spoken about the evening before or about Jamie's unexplained periodic hostility toward me, I felt safe and comforted by my sister. Yes, Trisha was like a mother to me.

9

The hanging of
Tommy LaPlante

1958

"Hey, Dad, do you mind turning down the volume on your tape recorder? I'm having a hard time studying!" I hollered down from the upstairs landing.

School was difficult for me—my concentration, poor. I never knew when I would come home from school to the stench of alcohol. Though I studied hard for every test, sometimes I still received a poor mark.

"You don't give a damn about my music, and I don't care about your studying!" Dad shouted back.

He made sure I heard him. I could hear him clomp across the floor as he moved toward the bottom of the stairs.

My hands clasped my burning cheeks. When I went back into my bedroom, I hurled my math books onto the double bed across from mine. I folded up the red vinyl-topped card table—my make-shift desk—and leaned it against the wall next to my closet. I walked to my dresser. On top of it, leaning against the mirror, was the beige leather shoulder bag my mother had given me for Christmas. As I opened the flap and brought the purse up to my nose, I inhaled deeply. It held the fragrance of love. I closed the flap and fastened it. Purse over my shoulder, I hurried determinedly down the stairs.

Tommy LaPlante[5]*—a murderer—he's the reason Dad got drunk this* *weekend. He cares more about a convicted murderer than he does about his own family. Tommy killed that man in cold blood—he did—it was all over the* Welland Tribune. *He bludgeoned him with a hammer. He's dead—hanged last Wednesday—January 16, 1958. He did it— the court proved him guilty! Dad has a hangover because of him...a murderer!*

He told Dad that he was innocent, and Dad believed him. That's all Dad has talked about since before and after Christmas.... "Tommy, he's innocent; he's just a kid." Ugh. Dad never should have taken that jail guard job. I heard Mom tell him so. Now, we have to listen to him rant and rave about Tommy!

"Where do you think you're going?" asked Dad.

He eyed me as I stepped out of the living room closet wrapped in my winter coat. "Stella's." I glared at him.

"Wipe that dirty look off your face."

Not a chance!

Stepping outside, I tentatively moved from the porch down the ice-encrusted back steps.

Whoa, I'm falling! Down the steps I skidded.

I reached up, grabbed the railing and pulled myself up from the bottom step. The melting snow penetrated the burgundy mittens that Aunt Olive had knit me for Christmas. My fingers felt cold; then numb. If only the cold could numb the pounding in my head.

10

The unwanted gift

1958

The blue bow uncurled as I pulled at the ribbon. Colourful paper, with "Happy Birthday" printed on it, covered a small square box. I unwrapped my gift and lifted the lid. I didn't know where to look or how to hide my displeasure.

Mom and Dad had been sitting in the kitchen drinking tea at our grey, chrome-trimmed Formica table. When I'd come into the room, both of them had sung "Happy Birthday" to me. My father, who liked to play the fool, had crossed his eyes while he sang in falsetto.

"How does it feel to be fourteen years old in your stocking feet?"

"Hardee, har-har-har, Dad," I'd managed to smile.

Mornings were the worst time of day for me. I felt out of sorts and crabby—birthday or no birthday.

I had seen my present on the table by the dish that held Dad's poached egg on toast—his usual breakfast choice. When I began tearing the wrapping paper off my gift, Mom picked up Dad's dish as well as her own breakfast plate and started to rinse them at the kitchen sink.

I stood staring at the delicate dress watch with the thin brown leather band. The crystal face was trimmed in gold. I couldn't lift my head. Holding back tears, I murmured, "Thank you," and continued to examine the watch's details. Although Dad *had* taken on some house-painting jobs after quitting his job at the jail, he couldn't afford such an extravagant gift. Even if he could have, the watch should have been given to Mom, whose birthday would follow five days later. I knew she wouldn't receive a gift from Dad, who had signed *his* name only on my card.

If you think you can win back my love by giving me an expensive gift, you can forget that!

I couldn't recall a time when Dad had given Mom a gift—not for her birthday, not for Christmas. But, Mom never failed to give one to him. She continued with her gift-giving, regardless, year after year.

The watch is pretty. Mom deserves to have it, not me.

"I have to go upstairs and get ready for work," Mom said as she dried her hands on her apron. She left the kitchen abruptly, without looking at the watch.

"Well, aren't you going to try it on?" Dad asked as he took the box from my hand. He removed the watch, grabbed my hand and fastened it on my wrist.

"Perfect fit," he said, grinning.

I lifted my arm and looked up at him. It was the prettiest object I had ever owned. It looked expensive, a real showpiece. *How surprised the girls would be! They wouldn't believe I could receive such a perfect gift. Too bad they'll never see it.*

A few days after my birthday, I was sitting at the kitchen table looking at the glass of Ovaltine Mom had left for me before she went to work. I stirred the brown flecks around in the glass, but I couldn't make them dissolve. *I hate breakfast!*

I looked toward the back door when Dad entered the kitchen. As usual, he had just dropped Mom off at the Four Square Gospel Church parking lot.

The Main Street bridge that loomed over the Welland Canal[6] was half a block from the church. No matter the season, in every kind of weather, Mom would walk across the bridge to work at Mitchell's Ladies' Wear. The store was another block and a half from the other side of the bridge.

Dad refused to take Mom further than the parking lot.

"Why the hell would I want to wait for the damn bridge to go up and down while a ship goes through, huh? Tell me that, will ya!"

There was no point in giving him the reason.

Dad pulled a chair out and sat opposite me at the kitchen table. "A few days before your birthday," he began, as he leaned his body over the table, "your mother found the watch that I gave you. She found it in the dresser drawer when she put away my socks. She thought it was for her."

I looked at him. He hadn't shaved for a couple of days. He smelled like a one-day-old uncooked piece of hamburger that hadn't been refrigerated. His flannel shirt had circles of perspiration stain under each arm.

Mom—the total opposite of Dad—was just about the cleanest person that I'd ever known. Everything and every family member had to be clean to her standard. Whenever Mom would get on Dad's case to take a bath, he would say, "The clean Brettells (Mom's maiden name) and the dirty Philps." It was as though he wrapped the two families in separate packages. I thought Dad's words rang true.

Grandma Philp seemed to have an undistinguishable odour about her—not like Dad's but kind of sickly sweet. Mom sometimes managed to persuade Dad to bathe when she told him just how bad he smelled. Fortunately, he listened to her. She didn't say it enough as far as I was concerned, but, then, why would Mom want to start World War III!

As Dad continued to talk, I got the feeling he was pleased with himself. *Has he done this as a mean prank on Mom, trying to make her jealous?* I said nothing. Lifting the glass to my mouth, I gulped the Ovaltine down, wiped my mouth on the sleeve of my cotton housecoat and left the kitchen.

My love for my mother had deepened as I became more aware of Dad's character. I witnessed her strength and her ability to endure a difficult marriage. I noticed the sacrifices she made for the family. Mom brought stability into our lives. She was unwavering in her dedication in keeping the family fed, clothed and churched. Dad contributed little. He always seemed to have his reasons for not working.

He had no business giving me a gift that rightfully belonged to Mom. I will NEVER wear the watch! I never did.

11

My high school years

1959-1963

"Claudia Philp, please step forward," said Miss Porter.

Height-challenged Miss Porter was the physical education teacher for the girls in grades nine and ten at Welland High. Her cheeks looked as velvety as violet petals but with an unremittingly crimson colour.

She smiled and glanced at me over the brown-framed glasses that rested on her ski-jump nose.

That day, four weeks into my first year of high school, I had been standing on the football field with thirty other grade nine and ten girls. My palms were wet. I bounced from one foot to the other, waiting. It wasn't the cold that caused me to jump up and down. I had been longing for this day.

"Stella Merwick stand next to Claudia," said Miss Porter, who now kept her eyes riveted to the chart she was holding.

I had had an adrenaline rush when my own name had been called. My confidence, on a good day, never measured up to Stella's.

"Hey, Stella," I shrieked jumping in the air for the second time. "Can you believe that we both made the cheerleading team?"

"No sweat, Philp," she said.

Whenever I heard my last name I felt like spitting. No one ever spelled it correctly. "Are you sure it's not spelled Philip?" I had been asked more than once. Besides, I shared the name with my father, and that didn't thrill me much ever since I found out about his drinking.

I stared straight ahead; then gave her a poke in the arm with my elbow.

"Don't call me Philp!"

Stella and I had been good friends since grade five. She expected to make the team because of her natural athletic ability.

My five-foot-two inch, blonde friend was popular with the boys. She had large, almond-shaped, blue-green eyes, full Elvis Presley look-a-like lips—without the sneer—and a heart-shaped face framed by short blonde hair. Her one unattractive feature was her wide nose with flaring nostrils, although she *did* get a couple of pea-sized, puss-filled zits every month too. Thankfully, I was spared those.

Stella was all about fun and boys. She wasn't the empathetic girlfriend in whom I could confide about my home life. No such friend existed throughout my teenage years. I had learned how to keep the family secret. My behaviour in social situations was the antithesis of the way I acted at home. I lived a double life. At home, I was inclined to be sullen and quiet. In social situations, I was outgoing and relatively popular. I tended to model my behaviour after Stella, though she was much more flirtatious and boy crazy.

Stella hadn't been invited to join either of the two sororities in town, while I had. The year after I was asked to join, I put Stella's name forward. Someone blackballed her. For membership, the vote had to be unanimous among the sorority sisters.

As a teenager in the late 50s and 60s, "going steady" had become a popular trend.[7] My guess was that the other sorority girls considered the shapely, sassy Stella, a threat—someone who could potentially entice a girl's boyfriend away.

When the cheerleaders travelled with the football team to an out-of-town game, we would first change from our school clothes into our cheerleading outfits. We wore cream-coloured pleated skirts with matching long-sleeved pullovers. A large, black felt "W" was sewn on the front of our sweaters. On the bus, some of the cheerleaders would stand resting their arms on the seat backs making conversation with the grinning teenaged boys. I hadn't honed the skill of flirting. It unnerved me as I watched some of the other girls chit chat with ease.

After we arrived at the school, we'd leap from the bus and run out to the field with our yellow and black, crêpe paper pom-poms in hand. We'd begin our chant: "We want a first down, we want a touchdown; first down, touchdown, man alive, grab that ball, raise that score; c'mon, Welland High, we want more!"

"Hi," said a voice across the aisle from me enroute to an "away" game.

I looked in the football player's direction. He had blonde hair, a brush cut and an engaging smile. Broad shouldered, even minus the shoulder pads, he stood about 5'8", with a solid physique.

"You're Claudia Philp, right?" he said.

"How'd ya know that?" I asked.

"I saw your picture in the paper last week. You know, the one that was taken of the junior cheerleaders," he said as he leaned over the arm of his seat. "My mother saw it, too. She said she thought you were Dora Philp's daughter."

"Your mother knows my mother?" I asked. *Wonder what his mother and he said about me.*

"Yup, she's known her for a long time. Your mother works at Mitchell's Ladies Wear, doesn't she?" he asked. I nodded. "That's where she met her. My mother makes sure your Mom waits on her whenever she goes into the store."

"By the way, I'm Bruce MacPherson. I was wondering...there's a dance in a couple of weeks. Would you go with me?"

I guess if his mom met my mother at the store, she doesn't know my father.

"Okay," I said while smoothing down my skirt.

"Are you sure?" Bruce said, as he began fiddling with the neckline of his navy blue sweater.

"This will be my first date. Let's meet at the high school."

"Okay, if you'd rather me not pick you up."

I didn't hesitate to tell him that it would be best if we met in the high school gym where the dance was being held. *If I can avoid introducing him to Dad, that's best.*

A week or so later, Mom and I had just finished doing the dishes together when the phone rang. She raised her eyebrows as she handed me the receiver. As I talked to the boy who had called, Mom skulked around the kitchen. She took a damp dishcloth and began moving the chrome canister set away from the wall—the back of the counter was wiped.

Like that needs cleaning!

Once that was finished, she went into the cupboard and began removing dishes. She walked over to the sink, rinsed out the *clean* cloth, came back to the cupboard—next to the phone—and wiped it down. The dishes clattered as she put them back in their place.

"Excuse me, Snooky," I said to the boy on the other end of the line.

I had met Martin (Snooky) Levy on the bus when our football team played Notre Dame High School. I thought he was a dreamboat—and exceptionally friendly—not in a flirtatious way at all. He had fine, sandy hair; his complexion seemed a little pale, but when he smiled, his dark brown eyes looked directly into mine.

I clamped my hand over the mouthpiece of the phone and whispered, "Mom, please, can't that wait 'til I'm finished talking?"

Mom put the last dish away. She removed her purse from the kitchen chair where it had been hanging by its strap since she came home from work. She took out her wallet and began rifling through its contents.

"Sorry, Snooky," I said.

As I pictured him in his football uniform, the heat rose to my cheeks. At the time I'd been introduced to him, I'd taken a liking to him. He appealed to me because as he spoke, he continued to smile. He didn't smirk like some of the other guys I had met.

"Would you go with me to the dance at the high school next Saturday night?" Snooky asked.

"Um-m, well, I already have a date." *Sugar! Why did I accept Bruce's invitation?*

"Okay. I'll call you again sometime," he responded before we hung up.

As I put the receiver back onto its cradle, Mom stood up at the table and pushed out her chair.

"I don't want you to think that I will ever approve of you going out with a Jewish, French or Roman Catholic boy. Who were you talking to on the phone?" she demanded, her lips pressed flat.

"Martin Levy, Mom," I said, twisting 'round and 'round on my finger the ring Trisha had given me two Christmases ago.

"Sounds like a Jewish name to me."

"I don't know. All I know is I won't be going to the high school dance with him. I'm meeting Bruce MacPherson there. His mother knows you from Mitchell's," I said as I lowered my head.

"Oh, May McPherson's son?"

"I s'pose."

"May goes to the Presbyterian church at the end of Bald Street. I'm sure Bruce is a nice boy. I like May."

"By the way, just so you'll know Mom, I'm quitting the junior girls' choir. I don't like Mrs. Rush. She's a grumpy, bossy choir mother. 'Hurry, hurry, hurry,' is all she says until we line up at the stairs in twos," I grumbled as I stalked off into the living room.

"You'll have to call her yourself, then. I'm not doing it for you."

"You won't?" I said as I stopped on the furnace grate and turned around.

"But you do everything for me, Mom."

"Not this time."

I shrugged my shoulders and plopped myself down onto the chair next to Dad. He lay on the couch watching *I've Got a Secret*.[8]

"Fine," I muttered. "I'm still quitting."

★ ★ ★ ★ ★

I sat and stared at the blackboard. My desk was one row and one seat over to the immediate left of where the sour-faced Miss Price sat.

"Claudia, I've thought about it," began my grade ten English teacher. She leaned over her desk and looked at me. "I've decided to give you a failing grade on your book report. I don't believe that you read the book."

I watched as her droopy jowls flapped back and forth when she shook her head.

"Cry, Claudia, cry," whispered Joanne, who sat behind me.

"I *did* read it," I said softly.

Pools of tears began to fill my lower eyelids—little reservoirs of water that stung. I wiped my right eye with my index finger. I felt woozy, dizzy.

I'm not a liar. I told the truth. I'm being punished for telling the truth.

My mind rushed through the lessons I'd learned about telling lies. From an early age, I knew lying was unacceptable to God. I sat in the choir pew for four years, close to the pulpit. I could see the minister spit when he got heated over some part of his sermon. There had been one message that came across clearly: "the Lord detests lying lips."[9] I never forgot those words, though much of what he said was soon forgotten.

That time I lied to Dad. He didn't find out until I fessed up.

I was riddled with guilt until I couldn't stand keeping it from him any longer. It was one of those compulsive lies. I purchased a couple of *Little Lulu* comic books with part of the money that Grandma Brettell had given to me for my birthday. Every year, I would receive a one dollar bill from my Mom's mother. When I returned home one day, Dad was sitting in the living room reading the *Welland Tribune.*

He put the newspaper down on the sofa and asked me what I was holding under my arm.

"Oh, just a couple of comic books I borrowed from Stella."

My immediate reaction had been to lie to him and yet, I knew I didn't need to. He would have been okay with my purchases. My reaction had been irrational, and it took me by surprise. Once said, I agonized over whether I should tell Dad or not. I even confessed the lie to my mother, who was down in the basement doing the washing.

"Go tell your father" Mom said. "If you lied, you have to tell him."

I plodded up the basement steps, moped through Grandma's kitchen—*Pee-yew! She must have had cabbage for supper!*—walked quickly through her doorway, then ours, to enter the kitchen. Dad was standing beside the gas stove, holding the tea kettle in his hand. Steam was rising from the spout.

As he poured the boiling water into the white china tea pot, I said, "Dad, I have to tell you that I didn't borrow those comics from Stella. I bought them. I don't know why I lied to you."

I couldn't look at him. My eyes remained riveted on my slippers. "I'm sorry."

His hand stopped in mid air. He looked at me, raising his eyebrows.

"Well, you better not do that again," was all he said and continued to pour the water into the teapot.

In his own way, Dad had forgiven me for lying to him. I made a promise to myself that I wouldn't lie from that day forward. However, I didn't realize, at the time, that in my sinful human condition, I was asking a lot of myself.

Lying—old lady Price thinks I'm lying—that I didn't read the book. Just like that time with the stale tarts. I've told the truth, yet I'm being punished. It isn't fair!

Five minutes before the bell rang for class to begin and before Miss Price made her pronouncement about giving me a failing grade, I had stood by the brainy Kathryn Murray's desk. I knew she had read the same book I had.

"I read that book you have on your desk," I said to Kathryn. "Did you like it?"

"Uh-huh."

"Me too, but I didn't know how to categorize it. Did you?" I'd enquired, feeling certain that she did.

Kathryn stared up me, shrugged her shoulders and said, "Sure, it was a human interest story."

What a dummy. Why couldn't I think of that?

I had jotted the information down on the sheet of paper, walked up to Miss Price's desk and handed it to her.

"Miss Price," I began, "I read the book, but I didn't know how to classify it. I *did* ask Kathryn Murray. She helped me with that part of the report."

The sullen Miss Price kept her head down while she looked over my paper. While I waited, I stared at the bald spot on the crown of her head. Her reddish-brown, kinky, thinning hair didn't conceal the area which was the size of a hen's egg.

"Sit down, Claudia. I'll have to decide how to grade you—*asking* Kathryn Murray!" She had made a sucking sound with her tongue.

"But I...."

"I said, sit down!"

She still thinks that I'm lying. What a horrible old hag. She doesn't know me; she doesn't like me!

The news that I would be given a failing grade penetrated slowly. I felt confused. I wanted to run—to escape the embarrassment of my classmates knowing that I failed.

Different—I'm different from everyone in this room. Just one more thing that makes me different.

I grabbed my school books and fled the room. Worried that I would be followed by Miss Price, I rushed toward the girls' lavatory—the closest door to the main doors where I would make my escape. School had become like another prison where I had to serve my time. I looked down at my scuffed black shoes. *Too tight!* For a few seconds, my pinched toes took the focus away from the pain of my preceding experience.

As I flung open the door of the washroom, the smell of disinfectant overwhelmed my senses. I began to cough and cry at the same time. I leaned against the mint green cement wall and shivered.

"Claudia, what's wrong?"

I looked up. My eyes couldn't focus through my mist of tears.

"Here, take this." A brown paper towel from the dispenser was offered.

"Thanks."

When I had dried my tears, I looked into the face of one of my sorority sisters—Dianne Bennett—so pretty with her clear skin, full lips and dynamic smile. I knew her to be popular and a good student. Resentment welled up.

"I'm quitting school!" I said. I turned and sprinted out of the washroom, ran toward the double doors, opened them and tore down the flight of stairs. I stood on the sidewalk for a few seconds. *Now what?*

* * * * *

It was 10:30 a.m. on Thursday. *Where will I go now?*

I stood at the corner of West Main Street and Denistoun realizing there was little choice.

Mom's at work. Shirley—likely at home—logical choice 'cause she quit school in grade ten. Won't work—neighbours could be there for coffee. Dad? Who knows where he is? Even if he's at home, it's out of the question. M-m-m, Dad always had compassion for the underdog...but no.

Decision made, I looked both ways and then crossed the street. Reaching into my school bag, I took out a Macintosh apple. I sunk my teeth into the skin and tasted the tender white flesh. The tart flavour was refreshing. The bile that had collected in my throat no longer held me hostage to the horror of my early morning encounter. I headed for Stella's house, one block from the high school.

Mrs. Merwick will be at home.

She was always home, often drinking thick black coffee while she sewed clothes for her two daughters. Mrs. Merwick sometimes sewed for women who preferred to employ a seamstress rather than purchase clothes that were often more expensive to buy off the rack. The off-the-rack garments were rarely made as well.

Chilly but sunny weather described this crisp November day. My feet shuffled through the dry, dark brown, dead leaves that covered parts of the sidewalk leading to 111 Bald Street where Stella lived with her mother, father and older sister, Jeanette. Mrs. Merwick—always kind to me—listened when I spoke. *She's the one to go to.*

I tramped up the asphalt driveway located to the left of Merwick's red-shingled, two-storey home. Mrs. Merwick was sitting at her sewing machine in front of the dining room window on the driveway side of the house. Her frizzy brown hair with streaks of grey had been tucked under a hair net and pulled back from her forehead. Short in stature, Mrs. Merwick was also a tad plump. She was a hospitable woman who always welcomed me into her home. She waved when she saw me. By the time I reached the back porch, my friend's mother stood at the door waiting.

"Here, give me dat apple core," she said as she held open her hand. She walked into the kitchen. I followed. The core went into a plastic container in the cupboard under the sink.

Stella's Mom said nothing but began to rinse out the coffee stained mug that sat on the counter near the porcelain sink. "Coffee first, talk second," seemed to be the household axiom. After drying the mug, Mrs. Merwick filled it with the black syrupy-looking liquid. No matter what she cooked, baked or fried, the smell of stale coffee filtered through the other aromas like the lingering smell of smoke after a fire.

I never tasted coffee before I met Mrs. Merwick. Someone once told me coffee stunted your growth. Maybe Mrs. Merwick was short because she started drinking it as a teenager. Stella's Mom also deep fried far too many donuts for the good of a person's health. I loved those donuts. As a young teenager, I didn't care a fig about whether coffee was good for me, or about coffee stunting my growth.

Mrs. Merwick's thick Hungarian accent often made it difficult for me to understand her. Sometimes, I had to ask her to repeat herself before I was able to "get it." My Dad would tell me to go wash out my ears if I couldn't understand what he said. It didn't happen often because we rarely talked.

"Sit down," Mrs. Merwick ordered. "Vhy aren't you in school?"

I took a gulp of coffee. *O-o-h, so bitter!* Still, the coffee was hot and comforting. I added more milk. She listened attentively as I proceeded to tell her what happened

"You can't quit school. Go tell your mother vat happened. Go, go now to the store, you havta tell your mother."

"Mom will *make* me go back to school. I want to quit. I can't go back there again," I sniffed. "I was humiliated."

"She won't do dat. She'll go vit you. Dat teacher was wrong vhat she did."

"My mother made me call Mrs. Rush when I wanted to quit the girls' choir. She wouldn't do it. She used to do everything for me, but now...."

"I think yur wrong. Dis is not the same ting. Here's yur coat, now go!"

Mrs. Merwick put her arm on my shoulder as she led me to the back door.

"Go!" she said as she gave me a gentle shove.

"Thanks for the coffee and donuts, Mrs. Merwick. Thank you for listening to me."

"Just go tell yur mother. She needs to know vhat happened. Don't quit school," she hollered after me as I descended the steps.

Glancing down at my Timex, I saw that it was close to noon. Mom had half an hour for lunch. Sometimes she would take it at twelve o'clock while at other times she would have to wait until one o'clock. It all depended on how busy it was at the store.

When I opened the front door of Mitchell's Ladies' Wear, tall, slender Mary Rutka greeted me with her big toothy smile.

"Hi Mary. U-u-m…you have lipstick on your front tooth." *Blah, blah. Do I ever think before I speak!*

She rubbed her middle finger vigorously back and forth over her two front teeth.

"Hope you don't mind me telling you," I said. "Sorry. Didn't mean to embarrass you."

"Oh, no, thanks. It must have been there since before I left for work."

I liked the ladies that my mother worked with. They were always asking me about school and how it was going with my boyfriend. Friendly would be the way I would describe each of them. Sometimes, I think they were like Mom's second family. She always spoke kindly of them. I think working at Mitchell's Ladies' Wear provided a degree of normality that contrasted with Mom's abnormal home life.

"What brings you here during the middle of a school day?" Mary asked.

Now what do I say? I don't want to lie.

"I just need to talk to Mom. It can't wait 'til she comes home."

"She's still upstairs in the bridal department. Go on up."

Sometimes I wondered whether Mom confided in her co-workers about Dad—or anything for that matter.

Mom's private. She holds everything inside. The women that she works with probably don't know a thing about her home life. She won't tell them about me, either.

The store was long and narrow. A rectangular glass counter located near the left front window, displayed gloves, hankies, costume jewellery and other accessories. Clothes hung on plastic hangers on each side of the maroon-and-blue speckled floor. I walked toward the stairs leading up to the second floor. Mom stood at the top with a brown lunch bag in her hand. When she looked down and saw me, she tilted her head to the side and frowned.

I waited for her to approach. She stopped on the step above.

"What brings you here? Why aren't you in school?" she challenged.

"Miss Price," I blubbered. "Mom, I hate school! I want to quit."

"S-h-h, keep your voice down. Stop crying. Here's a Kleenex."

Mom always seemed to have a Kleenex handy; either tucked under the sleeve of her sweater or behind the waistband of her skirt. While at home, she'd slip one down the front of her house dress between her ample breasts. I could count on Mom to be prepared for just about anything.

"Come upstairs," she said.

I kept my head lowered as Mom guided me toward one of the dressing rooms.

"Hi, Claudia," someone said.

"Keep your head down, it's Collette. Don't let her see you cry," Mom murmured.

Why did I come here? Mrs. Merwick was wrong!

"Hi Collette," I said while continuing to look at the floor.

Mom guided me into one of the dressing rooms and sat me down on the white wooden bench. She stood with her arms folded while she leaned against the light blue wall.

I gulped.

"Miss Price...she thinks I lied about the book I read, Mom! You know that I read it, remember?" Mom nodded. "She's going to fail me on my book report."

Bit by bit, I filled Mom in on the details. She didn't move to offer comfort. No arms reached out to touch or enfold me. I felt alone in my misery.

"I do remember...but you are not quitting school. Go home, now. I'll make an appointment with her. "*You'll* be going with me, Claudia."

The cords in Mom's neck became rigid; her sigh, heavy. One more burden added to an already arduous schedule.

"Aw, no. Ma...please don't make me go," I pleaded.

Mom opened the dressing room door—my cue to leave.

"Go home, now. I'm not going to make you go back to school until I have an appointment with Miss Price. Don't worry. *I'll* deal with Miss Price."

★ ★ ★ ★ ★

My mother didn't mention Miss Price again until Sunday evening when she told me that we had an appointment with her on Monday at 8:30 a.m. *sharp!* Mom explained to Miss Price that she had to make it to work by nine and intended to keep the meeting short.

I sat opposite Mom at the kitchen table that morning while she ate her standard breakfast of two pieces of toast *sans* butter but topped with orange marmalade. For a woman who watched her weight, I couldn't understand why she would eliminate butter and then go ahead and slather her toast with marmalade. I nearly gagged when I looked at the stringy-shaped bitter-tasting pieces of orange rind that I thought spoiled an otherwise tasty spread.

"Drink up, Claudia. It's 8:15. Go upstairs and clean your teeth. Let's get going," ordered Mom.

I took one last mouthful of my liquid breakfast and left the kitchen. I was proud of my mother—the way she dressed and carried herself. She had dignity and poise. Along with her other attributes, Mom was a no-nonsense woman. If my mother held an opinion contrary to another person's, she would hold her ground for what she believed to be true. How this would play out with Miss Price, I wasn't sure.

All weekend, thoughts darted through my mind like a mighty marathon of ants heading toward a trap from which there would be no return. I felt as though I could be imprisoned in a situation where life would be made even more miserable by the cantankerous, mean-spirited Miss Price. Preoccupied with thoughts of her reaction to a visit from my mother continued to make me apprehensive. Mom would *not* discuss with me what she would say, but I knew she would talk plenty.

"Believe you me, she's going to hear what I think!" I overheard Mom say to Shirley as she spoke with her on the phone on Sunday evening.

Pause.

"Something like that," said Mom in response to Shirley's query.

One thing I knew for sure, my mother was a determined woman. If she said she was going to say whatever she had told Shirley, I knew I wouldn't be disappointed. Nervous? Yes. But not disappointed.

"Are you ready to give the old bat what for, Dora?" Dad asked as Mom slid into the front seat of the car.

"Shush!" was all she said.

By the time Dad dropped us off at the high school, a cold wind had picked up. Mom got out of the car, then lifted her fox collar up around her ears.

I don't know how long my mother had saved for her grey herringbone wool coat with its expensive collar, but I did know that she could put items on lay-away at Mitchell's for months in advance. With this method of payment, plus an employee discount of ten to fifteen per cent, she was able to present herself as a well-dressed woman with impeccably good taste.

Throughout the seven minute car ride to school, I continued to cross and uncross my legs until my knees and calves started to burn. I sat in silence.

I want to get this over with. Please God make it be okay!

Mom opened the back door of the car.

"Hurry up! Why are you still sitting there?"

Despite my mother's urging, I slowly crawled out of the car. She grabbed my arm and gave a little pull.

"Mom...I don't want to do this. Can't I just wait for you in the hallway?"

Her face softened. "It'll be fine. You need to be there because I want Miss Price to tell you that she's sorry."

Thank you, God.

I felt better. Mom's love for her children had always been displayed by her actions, not often through words. Never had I heard the words, "I love you," spoken by my mother—or my dad, for that matter. Shirley once told me that whenever she was sick, she thought it was worth the suffering just to be taken care of by Mom. It was the only time she would ever call Shirley "dear."

* * * * *

It's difficult for me to remember the conversation Mom had with Miss Price that day. However, I *do* recall it was a *coup de grâce*!

While I sat and listened to Mom go at Miss Price, I experienced a spinning series of emotions. I had to bite my upper lip—so I wouldn't smile. My arms and legs shook, and I became breathless. At one point, I closed my eyes to savour the experience.

When Mom and I left the guidance office where we met with Miss Price, I walked with Mom to the main doors before going to class. Just as she was about to open the doors, I impulsively hugged her. My mother remained as stiff as one of the mannequins that she dressed at the store. However, before she walked out of the school, she turned, looked at me and said, "Good-bye, dear."

From that day forward, Miss Price was ever so kind to me. I had accepted her apology.

* * * * *

I looked toward the PA system and listened. The mention of my name made me cringe.

"These are your choices for the Students' Council for the 1961/62 school year," said Vice-Principal Mr. W. Box.

His first name was William, but behind his back students referred to him as Billy Box. No one liked him much. "Disagreeable" summed him up. Never smiling, he often gave out orders to the students as he approached them in the hallways during breaks.

"Don't come back to school tomorrow wearing those things," Mr. Box had said to me one late spring day. His white hair stood straight up from his scalp. He had plenty of it—a thick, coarse-looking mass on top of his head. It seemed as though he always wore the same grey suit—every day—year in and year out. Billy carried a perpetual sneer that looked overstated on his large, wide mouth.

Mom had purchased a pair of pink cotton culottes, as part of my new spring wardrobe. Culottes had been fashionable that spring. She had also bought me a striped pink, beige and white cotton blouse to complete my one spring ensemble. Culottes—A-line in style—resembled a skirt, except they were divided like a pair of trousers. Billy must have had up-to-date fashion magazines to flip through to know from a front view that I wasn't wearing a skirt. *The culottes came just below my knees, for Pete's sake. What was the big deal?*

Now, with the clicking sound of the intercom, we knew Billy was "off the air."

Did I hear him right? I've been nominated for Corresponding Secretary? Why would anyone nominate me?

I looked around the room at my classmates. No one that I could see had a look of surprise. Sylvia, the Italian girl who sat beside me in typing class, smiled broadly and winked at me. I didn't hang out with Sylvia. In fact, I didn't chum around with any of the girls in my class. Most of my friends were enrolled in General while I took Commercial with no plans to further my education once I finished high school. Most of the girls, upon graduation from General, became either teachers or nurses. I'd opted to take Commercial with the intention of becoming a secretary.

After the bell rang, indicating a fifteen-minute morning break, I watched Sylvia as she gathered up her books.

"Who nominated me, Sylvia?" I said.

"I got a bunch of the girls together, and we put your name forward."

"I don't think I'd be very good at being on the Students' Council." *My lack of confidence sticks to me like super glue.*

Sylvia's dark brown eyes were full of enthusiasm as she raised her eyebrows and touched my arm.

"Oh, you would, Claudia. You'd be so good!"

"M-m-m...nice of you to say so."

"You'll win. I know you will!" she said with all the enthusiasm of a cheerleader rooting for the home team. "Some of the girls and I are making signs to put up."

"Really?" I could feel my pulse begin to race. "I'm not sure that I want to get up in front of the whole school and make a speech. I know I'll have to do that," I said, feeling the moisture seeping through the underarms of my white cotton blouse.

"Make it short," said Sylvia.

"You can count on it!" *Yikes—in front of over 1,400 students.*

To my chagrin, and pleasure, I was voted in one day in May 1961.

★ ★ ★ ★ ★

When the new school year commenced the following September, my commitments hit me like the full thrust of wind from Hurricane Hazel.[10] I was battered by thoughts of having over-extended myself.

As well as being elected to the Students' Council, I had also been selected—for a third year—as a cheerleader; had accepted being asked to be on the Dance Committee; and had been elected as Theta Kappa Sigma sorority's Recording Secretary. Something had to go. Bruce, who had been my steady boyfriend for over a year, restricted my freedom. Even though most of my friends had boyfriends, I wanted to play the field and put my efforts into my commitments.

"But, I thought we were going to get married someday," said Bruce.

"Well I've changed my mind. I'm going to move to Toronto after I finish grade twelve."

Bruce looked down. He took my hand in his as we stood on the sidewalk outside my family's apartment. He leaned against the white clapboard and tried to draw me toward him. I pulled away.

"I'm sorry, Bruce."

I'd never witnessed a guy crying before. Without another word, I turned around, walked up the steps and into the house. Compassion wasn't high on my list of attributes.

Bruce had been the kind of guy I needed as my first boyfriend. He never asked why I didn't invite him over to my place. When we went to school dances, held about once a month, he would wait for me in our hallway, sometimes poking his head into the kitchen to say, "Hello" if he heard my parents' voices. Bruce would pick me up in his mother's royal blue Nash Rambler. Most Sunday evenings, I was invited to his home for dinner. His parents were kind to me and likeable. A feeling of mutual appreciation had existed between us.

Basically, my steady boyfriend was a nice guy—a person who could be trusted and someone who had expressed his love for me.

However, after I broke up with Bruce, I had an intense dislike for him. I considered him a sissy for having cried in front of me.

★ ★ ★ ★ ★

While peering at my reflection in my bedroom mirror above my dresser, I let down my hair from the elastic band holding it in a ponytail and began to brush it.

"Dad cut my bangs too short," I muttered. "I'm all forehead."

I'll just make a part on the right side of my head and let my hair fall along the left side of my face.

Once I finished fussing with my hair, I stood on my tiptoes to check out the rest of my appearance.

My peach-coloured, short-sleeved blouse, with the two pockets on either side, hid what wasn't there. *Not much hope for bigger breasts—already sixteen and still wearing a 32 A bra.*

I tucked my blouse into my matching gathered skirt and checked my appearance again.

"M-m-m...it'll do."

"Hi Dad, bye Dad," I said as I went soaring down the stairs.

That man needs a bath. Or some deodorant. Ugh. Puke.

Dad stopped at the top of the landing and spoke as though it were an afterthought.

"Where are you going?"

"Out with Nancy. We're going to a dance at the Guild Hall."

"Be home by eleven. While you're living under my roof, you'll live by my rules."

Right, Dad. When have I ever not lived by your rules?

"Sure, see ya."

Can't get out of here fast enough!

Nancy and I became friends after I broke up with Bruce. We were sorority sisters, cheerleaders together and attended the same place of worship: Holy Trinity Anglican Church.

A free spirit, Nancy hadn't wanted to be tied down to a steady boyfriend either. Stella had been out of circulation since grade ten. I'd lost her to a guy named Neil.

Holy Trinity held quarterly dances for young people at the Guild Hall—a large room on the second floor annex connected to the church.

This was the place where the Sunday school classes were taught weekly. At eight years of age, I'd taken tap-dancing lessons in the Guild Hall.

December 31, 1960, was the last time I'd attended a dance at the Guild Hall. My classmate, Sandra Leishman, and her boyfriend, who had also been at the dance, were asphyxiated sometime after midnight while parked on a city side-street.

It was assumed that Sandra's twenty-one-year-old boyfriend had left the motor running to keep the car warm. Obviously, he hadn't realized the tailpipe had settled into a snowbank by the side of the road. The couple had been found early the next morning huddled together in the front seat of the car—Sandra was dead and her boyfriend, barely alive. He never regained consciousness and died a few days later.

Two days after New Year's, Miss Legree sat on the corner of her desk holding the list of names of her grade ten typing and shorthand students. Each teacher was required to take roll call before the first class of the day began.

Diminutive in stature and severe in manner, Miss Legree began calling out the students' names in alphabetical order.

"Sandra, Sandra L.?" she said while scanning the room.

Silence.

"Sandra? Does anyone know where Sandra is?" she asked.

"She's dead," piped up one of the two boys in the class.

Miss Legree turned white.

"She's dead?" Her dull, greenish-blue eyes looked down at the list of names.

"Oh," she said. "Kathryn M.?"

"Here," said Kathryn.

Eventually Miss Legree said the name of Sandra's best friend— the girl she always walked with to class.

"Violet S. Is Violet here?"

No one helped her out on that one. We left *her* to figure it out.

★ ★ ★ ★ ★

From the other side of Main Street, I watched Nancy waiting for the stoplight to turn red. In constant motion, she snapped her fingers and swayed to the beat of the music that played in her head. When she took leave of her reverie, she spotted me and waved vigorously. Before I knew it, she was beside me, grabbing my hand and running toward the Main Street bridge. We could see a cargo ship approaching down the canal. If we didn't hurry, we would be fifteen minutes late for the dance that was to begin at 7:30 p.m.

Nancy's thick black hair hung in chunks of curls below her ears. Her dark complexion and brown eyes made her look Italian. She didn't resemble either of her parents. Although her mother's hair was mostly white, she had skin the colour of buckwheat flour. Her father, also pale in complexion, had a roadmap of wrinkles on his face. He seemed to be more the age of a grandfather than the father of a teenager.

I thought Nancy might have been adopted until one of the girls in our sorority sat gossiping about her on the steps of the high school one day following classes.

"Do you know that Nancy's sister is really her mother?" Sandy asked.

"Well, no, how do *you* know that?"

"My mother told me. She remembers when it happened. Her sister met this Italian guy at a dance and got pregnant. The sister's mom sent her off to a home for unwed mothers. After she had Nancy, her 'sister' never went back to her parents' house. She moved out; then married some guy named George. My mom's friend knows Nancy's mother. That's how I know. I bet your mother knows, too. It was the talk of Welland."

Mom had not been one to gossip. I never overheard a conversation where she talked about someone else's problems.

"C'mon Sandy," I said giving her a playful swat on the arm. "Why would you joke about something like that?"

"You don't believe me?" Sandy said as her hand flew to her chest.

I don't want to believe her. There are no secrets in this town! Everyone probably knows my Dad's an alcoholic.

"Does Nancy know?"

"No idea…don't imagine so. What good would it do for her to know about that?"

And what good does it do for us to gossip about our friend?

"But it is okay that everybody else knows?" I mumbled. "I gotta go. See you, Sandy."

I headed home. My thoughts were spinning. Gene Pitney's song, "Town Without Pity" popped into my head: "*When these little minds tear you in two….*"[11]

* * * * *

Dating during those years translated into attending Saturday matinees and school, church or service-club sponsored dances in the region. Drive-in movie theatres, or "passion-pits" as they were called, were a popular place for couples who wanted to make out. Most of the girls I hung around with stayed away unless they were double-dating.

Some of the girls who went steady ended up pregnant. Most of those who did get pregnant were married by the time they were sixteen or seventeen. Sandra L. had been only sixteen when she died. Had she been headed for pregnancy and marriage?

Finding a deserted road to park on or babysitting was a form of entertainment for steadies. Parents seemed to be confused as to what constituted a watchful eye on their teenage progeny. If a curfew was in place and the teen kept to the set time, parents seemed to have the idea that their teens could be trusted to behave.

A fun loving girl with a Natalie Wood smile, Nancy's upbeat, cheerful disposition affected me like a cool breeze after a hot summer day. Being with her both soothed and invigorated me.

"Did I tell you that I plan on moving to Toronto when I'm finished school?" I asked. "Wanna come?"

Nancy stood before the rectangular mirror in the washroom of the Guild Hall. She put down her comb.

"Really—you're going to move to Toronto?"

Nancy looked down. Her shoulders drooped.

Seconds later, she said "I'm going into nursing in Niagara Falls. I've been planning to become a nurse for a long time. I really want to do this." Her smile broadened. We both had another year of school to complete before we would be going our separate ways.

The door to the washroom swung open.

DooDoo Simons walked in. This slender, reddish-blond-haired girl lived on the other side of the tracks, East Main Street. She was a tough teenager who usually dressed in short skirts and tight sweaters. Skinny and of average height, DooDoo was actually quite pretty, although her large lower lip seemed to be fixed in a perpetual pout. A faintly bitter scent accompanied her as she walked by us. The smell reminded me of a smouldering log. Doo-Doo dated a guy who wore his hair in a duck tail—greasers—we called guys like him. Whenever I saw them together, her boyfriend had a cigarette perched on the upper part of his right ear.

"Hi, chicks," said DooDoo.

We both nodded a greeting and watched as she entered the stall.

Silence.

Smoke soon began to rise above the green wooden door of the stall DooDoo had entered. "If Miss Whitson finds out, she'll kick her out and won't let her come back," Nancy whispered. I nodded in agreement.

The dances held at the Guild Hall were chaperoned by various adults—one man and one woman. Some were parents, others teachers. Miss Whitson was one of the few teachers I liked while in high school. She was kind, helpful and taught in an interesting manner, a way that helped a student to remember the facts.

Nancy looked at me, "Let's get out of here. They've started playing the music,"

"*I said come on over baby, a whole lotta shakin' goin' on,*"[12] she sang.

I flipped up the beige leather flap of my purse, popped in the tube of pearly-pink lipstick, closed the flap, put the strap over my shoulder and followed Nancy out of the washroom. Tossing our purses onto the nearest folding chair, then, holding hands, we bopped out onto the dance floor. I let Nancy lead. She lifted up her arm for me to spin under it, all the while we bounced on the balls of our feet. Back and forth...hands together...hands apart... another twirl. Exhausting but exhilarating!

The only guys dancing were the ones who had girlfriends. Most likely, they learned to dance because their steadies taught them. Some fellows looked awkward, as though dancing didn't come naturally. If they felt self-conscious, they would stand around and watch the girls dance together—until a slow song began to play. By the time an upbeat song ended, they would have scanned the room and selected the girl they hoped to hold close.

Nancy and I were content to dance with each other most of the time. If we *were* asked to slow dance with a guy, we rarely refused the first time but a second invitation we declined. There was no desire to give encouragement. We weren't about to lead a guy on, to have him think we were particularly interested in him.

Dates with guys came and went through the remaining year-and-a-half of high school. For a short time, I dated two different fellows—at two different times. Essentially, playing the field was by far more appealing.

Following grade twelve, I was hired in June to work as a stenographer in the personnel department of Page-Hersey Tubes in Welland.

One year later, Shirley drove me to Toronto for a job interview. I'd answered an ad in *The Telegram* (a now-defunct Toronto newspaper). I was hired on the spot.

* * * * *

My friends all had different plans: Stella had become engaged to Neil; Nancy had gone into nursing; another friend, Janie, had opted for Teacher's College. I was on my own with my dream of leaving Welland.

In 1965, six months after I moved to Toronto, Grandma Philp died. Dad and Mom took over the main part of the house. They rented out the back apartment where we had lived. My parents had discussed this arrangement previously with Grandma, Dad's sister, Dorothy and his brother, Lionel. The stipulation of leaving the house to Mom and Dad, upon Grandma's death, was for Aunt Olive to continue living there. Being legally deaf since birth, Aunt Olive had never been gainfully employed but had lived with my grandparents. When Grandpa died, she took care of Grandma who suffered for years with congestive heart failure.

Mental illness seemed to be pervasive in the Philp family. Not only did Grandpa Philp die in a mental institution, but on one occasion, Aunt Olive became so excessively distraught over some undisclosed incident, that she slit her wrists with a razor and was hospitalized. As a result, Aunt Olive was prescribed medication for depression.

Mom and Dad took on a huge responsibility with the care of Aunt Olive. Eventually, she had to be placed in a group home. Her mood swings had kept Mom and Dad on edge. Dad's siblings agreed—they knew how difficult Aunt Olive could be.

12

Escape to the big city

1964-1965

I arrived at the bus terminal in Toronto late one Sunday afternoon.
Mom had made me a thick ham sandwich, slathered in mayon-
naise, topped with lettuce. She worried that I wouldn't be able to
buy groceries on a Sunday. In my brown lunch bag, she included
a large slice of her lemon cake topped with a thin drizzle of icing,
and an apple. By the time I arrived in Toronto, the bag was empty.

During the fifties, my sister Shirley had lived in a brick,
three-storey rooming house for women on St. George Street, the
hub of "fraternityland." In 1964, I moved into the same house.
Apart from the young women who occupied the rooms, nothing
had changed. Mr. and Mrs. Wilson, a retired couple, owned the
building. A squat little woman named Simy was still the house-
keeper. In the evenings, there was a constant buzz of chatter, the
opening and closing of bedroom doors and the incessant ringing
of the doorbell.

Mr. Wilson was particularly strict regarding his rules. "There is
to be no loitering in the vestibule with your dates. If there is, I'll
ring the buzzer," Mr. Wilson had warned.

The day I arrived, there was little activity on the streets of
Toronto as the taxi drove me to my new home. Already, I was
beginning to feel a little homesick. When I walked up the wooden

steps, rang the doorbell and was greeted by the Wilsons, their smiles warmed me.

As I stepped from the foyer into the hallway, Mr. Wilson took the suitcase from my hand. He puffed his way up the winding staircase located to my right. The visible interior of the house was trimmed in oak, much like my Grandma Philp's house. On the left of the spacious hall, French doors led into what appeared to be a library. The doors' windows were covered over with heavy brown drapes. Mrs. Wilson walked toward the room and lightly tapped on one door with her knuckles. The door opened.

"Gaye McAvity, I would like you to meet Claudia Philp. She's our new resident."

"Hello, there!" said the friendly, black-haired girl.

I liked Gaye immediately. She opened her door further in a welcoming gesture. Wall shelving confirmed that a library *had* been converted into a bedroom.

Gaye's shiny, thick, dark hair fell into a flip around her shoulders. Like me, she had blue eyes—more striking on a girl with such dark hair. Freckles lightly covered her pale cheeks. Her impish grin gave me the impression she liked to tease.

"I want to introduce Claudia to you before she goes upstairs to her room. I don't think any of the other girls are at the house right now," explained Mrs. Wilson.

"C'mon down after you finish unpacking," invited Gaye.

I smiled and nodded.

Mrs. Wilson took me into a large, square-shaped kitchen down the hallway from Gaye's room. The walls had been painted off-white. Dotted Swiss sheers were gathered evenly along a shiny rod on the single rectangular window facing the backyard. Clustered around a sizeable yellow wooden table were ten spindle-back wooden chairs with colourful seat cushions.

"The girls use the kitchen for their meals. No set hours. They come and go as they please. It's worked out well, so far."

Mrs. Wilson led me to the refrigerator, opened it and showed me which shelf was assigned to me. Each food item had to be labelled with full initials. A black marker was placed next to the fridge for that purpose. Cupboard space was also provided. Mrs. Wilson showed me my assigned shelf. The same marker was to be used for non-perishable food items. I was told that the marker had to be tucked back into the wooden pencil holder beside the fridge.

She's organized, just like Mom!

Feeling a lot better, I went up the stairs with this most pleasant landlady. She showed me the faded cream-coloured bathroom that had a toilet, two towel racks, a small mirror above the sink and a white porcelain tub with clawed feet—reminiscent of my grandma's bathroom at home. It was adequate, as far as I was concerned. There were no towels on the racks. I assumed we were expected to keep them in our rooms. I was told I would be sharing the bathroom with five other gals.

Five females? No stepping into dribbles around the toilet!

Mrs. Wilson handed me the list of "Rules for Residents" before opening the door to my room.

"Thank you, Mrs. Wilson."

"Your roommate, Carol Crocker, should be back sometime this evening," she said. After backing out of the bedroom, she gently closed the door.

My speckled brown cardboard suitcase with the dark panels down the middle lay on the bed nearer the window. Having shifted my luggage, I stretched out on the soft mattress of the twin bed. *Feels just like home.* The light blue cotton curtains were draped on each side of the window, held back with a band of the same material. I was startled to see another brick house only one foot away through the glass.

Up again! Time to unpack.

The top of a mahogany dresser beside the closet was slightly marked with two faded circular rings the size of a teacup. On the left side of the dresser, neatly placed, were my roommate's toiletries. I removed my makeup and deodorant from my blue-and-white flowered plastic cosmetic bag and set them on the right side. Two of four large dresser drawers were empty. *I'll only need one.*

After putting a few sweaters, underwear and my full-length nylon slip away, I closed the drawer. The closet was narrow. I hung my two skirts up with clothespins on the wire hangers provided. Closing my suitcase, I slid it under the bed. After kicking off my shoes, I swung my legs onto the light pink chenille bedspread, lay down and closed my eyes.

I like this place. I wonder if Carl and his family are over for dinner tonight. It's Sunday—I bet they are. Why am I thinking about this? I'm going to make myself homesick.

With two women assigned to each room, there was no choice as to my roommate. The possibility of my not liking her hadn't occurred to me. Girlfriends were important to me. My social life depended upon the connections I had to other young women.

My first roommate, Carol, hailed from Wawa, Ontario. She was a tall, blonde, hippie girl with a big smile. Her beehive hairstyle, beautifully coiffed each morning before she left for work, completed her stylish appearance. Three months after I moved in with Carol—who rarely stayed at the house on the weekends—she made an announcement.

"Derry and I are getting married at the end of the month," she said one Monday evening.

"Married? Didn't you just get back with him?"

"He's the guy I want. Why wait?"

Getting married at twenty—not for me!

★ ★ ★ ★ ★

Gaye and I became good friends. However, she had a boyfriend—her roommate didn't. I liked Patricia but she was a little too serious to be a close friend of mine. No connection there.

For a while, I became a party girl—in the sense that I loved to dance and would attend frat parties when invited. When the guys from the fraternity across the street were throwing a bash, the first invitation would be extended to the women living in our residence. We provided an abundant supply of dancing partners. The university men exuded the confidence that had eluded the teenage boys from Welland. Transition from high school to university, plus maturity, more than likely attributed to the differences. Whether they could or couldn't jive, jitterbug or do some modification of a waltz, they danced. The slow beat of "The House of the Rising Sun"[13] played repeatedly until I knew every word by the third or fourth frat party.

By spring 1965, I had had my fill of going unaccompanied to fraternity parties. Dave and I, one of the guys who lived at the frat house, began dating shortly after we met at one of the parties. Dave was about 6'3" with a thin face and a long, straight nose. He wore his black hair closely cropped. What attracted me to Dave was the fact that he had a dry sense of humour and a large dose of self-confidence. Once we began dating, I would go with him to the Wednesday night parties across the street.

One evening, as Dave and I walked through the entranceway of the frat house, a pungent smell hit me smack in the face. A heavy, thick, skunk-like odour permeated the air. I had smelled beer before, but not on my Dad, he only drank cheap wine. My first encounter with the foul stench had been at the home of my Uncle Jack, my mother's alcoholic brother. The frat boys usually had beer at their parties, but the smell had never been as strong as it was on that particular night.

Dave and I began dancing as soon as we entered the living room. The scuffed-up wooden floors were well-used for dancing. When "Bits and Pieces"—the 1964 hit song sung by the Dave Clark Five—began to play, all the guys would stand in one place and stamp their feet to the beat of the chorus, just as the Dave Clark Five did when performing.

Someone was calling my name from the other room. Dave held my hand as we walked toward the hallway.

"Look up the stairs, Claudia," said an unfamiliar male voice.

I froze on the spot when I glanced up; then screamed as I grabbed on to Dave's arm.

At the top of the stairs stood a guy with dark blue jeans and underwear lying in folds at his feet. He glanced over his shoulder and down the stairs. Then, he bent over and exposed his bare bottom. *Disgusting.*

I clenched my teeth. "Get me out of here, Dave."

Dave explained that the guy was visiting from a brother fraternity in London, Ontario. He didn't know him and thought he was ignorant for doing what he did. Still, Dave didn't say anything more. He walked me to the door of the fraternity house. I ran down the steps, across the street and went up the stairs to the safe haven of my room.

I didn't date Dave much after that incident. *How did that stranger know my name if Dave hadn't told him?* From one of his frat brothers

I found out that Dave had a girlfriend, a stewardess, who was often not around. No way was I going to be played for a fool or be some guy's part-time sweetheart! It had been easy for him to date me during the week while she was away. Most weekends, I travelled home to Welland.

Despite the fact that I had looked forward to leaving home, once I lived in Toronto I was homesick. Taking the bus to Welland on Friday night became a weekly occurrence during the first four or five months. I'd leave by bus on Friday evening and return to Toronto on the 6 a.m. train Monday morning. Dad would get up early and drive me to the station. For the most part, the weekends would be spent visiting Shirley and some of my old friends. Sometimes, at noon on a Saturday, I would walk across town and over the bridge, arriving at Mitchell's to take Mom out for lunch at the café across the street.

My relationship with Dad had improved once I moved out of the house. I would even take the chance of being home knowing I might have picked the same weekend he would choose to go on a bender. The desire to see my mother outweighed my fear of Dad's binges. I knew I could always return to Toronto earlier than planned. It seemed, however, that when Dad knew I was coming home, he refrained from drinking.

"Are you almost ready for me to take you to the train station, Claudia?" Dad would holler from the bottom of the stairs.

"Give me two minutes and I'll be down."

Our "good-byes" were always brief. I wouldn't hug him. Dad appeared to know how I felt about him. He would hang back after handing me my suitcase before I boarded the train.

"Thanks for the ride, Dad."

"Coming home next weekend?" he sometimes asked.

"I'll see. I'll call if I am."

How melancholy was the sound of the whistle blowing as the train moved slowly out the station.

I wish I could hug Dad.

I pictured him driving back through the dark streets of Welland, across the Lincoln Street bridge, over the tracks, winding his way home. Maybe he would be thinking about the daughter who never showed him love.

It must have wounded my father when I wouldn't give him a hug, but I never thought about *his* feelings, only my own and then my mother's. I felt that I had deserted her by moving out of the house and away from Welland. Although she never tried to hold me back, I didn't have any idea how my mother really felt about my leaving. She continued to keep silent about her feelings and all things that were difficult for her.

By 1965, I had changed jobs and begun working at The Hospital for Sick Children. I moved up from the position of stenographer to secretary for two neurologists.

My day-to-day life, from Monday to Friday, was spent working from 9 a.m. to 5 p.m. I made friends with the women who worked in the same office. Visits home became less frequent as my friendships in Toronto became solid and dependable.

13

Meeting Chuck

1967

The door opened with a bang. All heads turned away from the art instructor who had begun his life-drawing class at 8 p.m. sharp. He folded his arms and leaned first on one leg and then on the other. He remained silent, his face expressionless.

It was an October evening in 1967. I was a newcomer, taking an art class to compensate for the one I missed the week before. My dad's artistic talent had been shared with my two sisters. Art also interested me, so I had decided to enrol in the Three Schools of Art to see whether or not Dad's gift had been passed on to me.

All eyes focused on the lanky, blonde, good-looking and, seemingly, self-confident young man. He grabbed a bench in order to take his place with the other students; then, nodded and smiled at our instructor. His smile was not returned.

Wish this guy would find himself a seat and sit down somewhere. H-m-m-m, he may look good but he's blatantly rude!

The evening's class was crammed with fourteen adults—twelve men and two women. I watched as the guy scanned the faces of the students.

Uh-oh, here he comes.

I looked at the fellow with the red hair and brush cut sitting next to me.

"Would you move over, please? I'd like to put my bench here," said the interloper. Red initially seemed reluctant but gave a snicker and then, complied.

I can't believe this guy asked him to move. There's barely any room between us and he's squeezing himself in. He's so distracting, totally lacking in finesse.

I glanced over my shoulder at him. I was feeling uncharitable and did not return his smile.

My boyfriend, John, and I recently decided on a trial separation in order to further examine our commitment to one another. It had been his idea. I was hoping our relationship would end in marriage. I missed him and found that I was intolerant of the shortcomings of men.

Without an apology, the blonde guy sat down and proceeded to lean in toward me.

"Hi! I'm Chuck. Have I missed much?" he whispered.

"Ten minutes worth and about three minutes of what we may have learned while you scanned the room."

I hesitated to say more but added, "I'll give you my notes at the break."

"Hey, thanks!" said Chuck.

H-m-m. He does have some measure of manners.

The instructor resumed his lecture until break time.

I was about to rise from my bench when I felt Mr. Oh-So-Suave lean into me again. This time, I managed to feel a little more benevolent toward him as we engaged in a few exchanges regarding the lecture. It was unlike me to remain disgruntled over a minor incident of inconvenience.

Suddenly, he blurted out, "I bet you're here looking for a boyfriend."

Where did this come from?

For the first time, I turned and faced him directly. I caught the stunning brightness of his blue eyes—cool pools of vivid colour. I was unexpectedly charmed by his mischievous grin and the unique and engaging way he attempted to flirt. He had undeniably garnered my attention with his last comment.

"Huh!" I chuckled. "That's really novel...it's a good one."

"So, would you like to go out for a drink with me after the class?" asked Chuck.

"Sure—why not."

★ ★ ★ ★ ★

Chuck and I dated two or three times before John and I got back together. Although I enjoyed Chuck's company, my heart still belonged to someone else.

14

Not according to plan

1969

As I lay on Mom's bed—back in Welland—curled up in a ball, facing the radio she had given me for my birthday, I hummed to the lyrics of Roy Orbison's song, "Only the Lonely."[14]

It was January 1969. I had been dating John since April 1967. At the time we met, I wasn't looking for a boyfriend, but I had grown weary of dating. There was a party—I liked his smile; I liked that he seemed truly interested in me. Short-term relationships with a variety of men had been shallow. I felt as though I was on a treadmill, in constant motion but going nowhere.

There were no plans to move back to Welland. Yet, here I was, back at home. After dating John for eighteen months, we became engaged. One month later, John broke off the engagement.

"I love you, but I can't marry you." At the time, I felt deeply hurt and confused. It wasn't until my life changed through faith that I realized God had another man, a Christian man, chosen for me to marry.

★ ★ ★ ★ ★

I had been studying at the Children's Psychiatric Research Institute, in London, Ontario, to become a child care worker. John had gone back to the University of Western Ontario to get his M.B.A.

My stay was short. I bolted from the rooming house where I had been living, without even giving notice to the Centre. When and how had I become so irresponsible?

My mundane life was dissatisfying. Before I met John, I thought nothing of standing up a date. Several times I wasn't even there to answer the knock at my door. Sometimes, I would decide to go to a movie with a roommate, never disclosing that I had a date I had no intention of keeping. The men didn't call back. I didn't care.

Now, during the bitter cold days of late January, I was back at home.

I heard Dad's footsteps as he trudged up the stairs. Swinging my legs over the edge of the wrought iron double bed, I grabbed a Kleenex. Dad peered into the room. I broke into sobs, walked over to him and flung my arms around his neck. He held me while I let the tears flow onto the shoulders of his blue and white plaid flannel shirt.

"Dad, this hurts so bad!" I wailed.

"I know...I know," he sniffed.

His shoulders began to heave. The pungent odor of perspiration hit my nostrils. I took a step back. He reached into his trouser pocket and handed me his wrinkled handkerchief. I handed it back to him. Dad blotted his eyes. I blew my nose into the tear-soaked tissue I held clenched in my hand.

"What's the matter with that guy, anyway. I'm gonna call him!"

"No, don't," I implored. "We're through."

Suddenly, I felt embarrassed by the overt display of emotion between us. With his eyes downcast, Dad turned and left the room. I heard him quietly close the door to his bedroom.

★ ★ ★ ★ ★

Mom was a strong support after John broke up with me. I didn't have a job and, therefore, no money. She offered to cash in a life insurance policy in order for me to go away on a vacation. Mom shared her double bed with me. Even through her loud snoring, I felt comforted by being physically close to her. I stayed with Mom and Dad for a week, before moving into an apartment with my girlfriends in Toronto.

After two weeks, I was in "flight mode" again. I wanted to be with Trisha to escape from my misery. My *modus operandi* seemed to be to run, thinking that was the answer. I wanted to escape from any situation that had a negative impact on my psyche.

During this time, I called Chuck. I told him what happened between John and me, and he invited me out for lunch.

"You know, time heals all wounds," he had said. "But, time also wounds all heels."

"M-m-m...you really think so?"

I liked the idea of some kind of sweet revenge—that John would want me back, and I wouldn't be available.

Mom purchased an airline ticket to Oromocto, New Brunswick, for me. That's where Trisha and Bill lived with their three daughters and son. Chuck drove me to the airport.

15

On the run again

1969

My stay with Trisha was short-lived. Three weeks after my arrival, I was on the train from Fredericton back to Toronto. I wanted out. My girlfriends had been notified, and the four of them were ready to share their apartment with me. My bed—the living room couch.

I hadn't felt any different at Trisha's than I felt at home. What made me think I could run away from my pain? Why did I think Trisha wouldn't have her own problems once she left home? Had I even considered that she might not be leading a perfect life? I shuddered as I remembered that night....

Heavy footsteps thumped up the stairs. My brother-in-law's silhouette passed by my second-floor room. A few minutes later, Bill was standing in the doorway of the bedroom. He staggered over to me.

"Where's my son?" he slurred, his face two inches from mine. Having just returned from the officers' mess, Bill was dressed in his Black Watch uniform. Trisha was out playing bridge at a friend's house in the neighborhood. I had been left to babysit.

The sour stench of alcohol orbited the air around my head; drawing me into a vortex of past horrors. I pulled up the bedsheet and clenched it close to my chin.

Dear God—don't let him hit me.

His twisted mouth spewed saliva as he spoke.

"Jamie called me from his friend's house and asked me. I'm sorry. I didn't know he couldn't stay over. I didn't know he wasn't allowed." Shaking uncontrollably, I began to whimper.

"Don't do it *again!*"

After his shrill directive, Bill staggered out of the bedroom.

I was on a cot in a room with my nieces—one four years old and the other eight. If they heard anything, they didn't let on. I rolled onto my stomach and burrowed my head into my feathered pillow. My quiet snivelling continued until I drifted off to sleep.

The next day I told Trisha I would be moving back to Toronto. Once again, I was on the run.

Initially, it had been my intention to find a secretarial job in Fredericton and live in Oromocto for an indefinite period of time. Bill and Trisha both seemed fine with the idea. I had been looking for one week but received no job offers.

I had received a letter around March 1st, from Chuck. It arrived shortly after I sent him a "thank you" note for taking me to the airport. It made me consider the friendships I had acquired in Toronto. I would not return to Welland to live.

★ ★ ★ ★ ★

February 25, 1969

Dear Claudia,

I was surprised and pleased to hear from you so soon. I have always guarded my letter writing habits rather jealously and therefore, if you knew me better you should be equally surprised to hear from me (but of course we can always chalk it up to hidden psychological motives!)

I wrote a good law exam on Friday. On Saturday, I went home for the weekend to meditate about my future. I think I was depressed on Friday night but after the weekend of solitude and reflection, I've regained an aggressive and confident attitude about the whole situation, viz. that I know I can survive and be good on my own and that no matter what the situation in Toronto, it is wrong for me to take the attitude that it is a personal failure to

NOT be able to get a job in Toronto. I also found out today there are approximately 50 guys looking for a job in TO and that makes it even more realistic (the rationalization, I mean). In any case, I had an interview today, but I was honestly told that they are interviewing a number of applicants—so I won't know for a while about the result. Also, I have further explored an association with a friend in the T.D. Centre and will learn his thoughts over lunch on Wednesday.

My younger brother, Al, got a bit of a shocker thrown at him last week: his fiancé just started dating other guys and when pressed for details told him she just wasn't sure anymore—so I guess good-bye engagement and goodbye August wedding. So you see, people from both sexes can do funny things and that the old problem of "what is love?" is never solved until the whole thing has been confirmed and reconfirmed in marriage. But, I don't think it means that people are always taking a big chance before getting married—because, I think now that mutual desire to get married is, in fact, a true declaration of love if it is genuine. So, therefore, the only problem is determining genuineness in a person. So much for the lecture.

You know, I do regret New Brunswick being as far away as it is mostly because I think we were only getting to know each other (maybe understand each other) very recently. That is one of the reasons I said that I enjoyed a week ago Saturday because on Thursday night, I told you about certain things (and even blasted you for it) and on Saturday, we joked about the same thing. I got the impression that maybe you had understood what I had tried to say and yet, it didn't make the parting any more difficult or strange—because it was realistic.

Like some famous psychologist once said, "If there was perfect communication, there would be perfect understanding and therefore, no wars." Aha—maybe we briefly touched on perfection (re communication) for a day—or maybe that's just wishful thinking on my part.

I hope you're getting some skiing in, gaining ten pounds, earning some money, taking good care of your nephew (and nieces?), not running away and getting married with some "Newfie," going to church every Sunday, brushing your teeth after every meal, forget-

ting (and even forgiving) John, turning Oromocto upside down with your dazzling presence, boosting my ego and writing me occasionally, not quitting any jobs without proper notice, and not forgetting Ontario is still the centre of Canada. (I hope you don't get old reading this letter.)

Chuck

On the train back to Toronto, I reflected on the past year, pausing to remember the August 1968 wedding of mutual friends, Lynn and Preben.

While John and I had sat side by side in the church pew, I watched Chuck, the best man, take his position at the front of the church. Dressed in a black tuxedo, he stood leaning on one leg as he waited for the bridal procession to begin.

M-m-m...when I look at him, I think of a long, cool refreshing drink of lemonade: his stature, his sun-bleached hair, the leanness of his physique, his forthrightness. What am I doing sitting next to this man that I think I want to marry? He is too quiet. I never quite know what he's really thinking.

* * * * *

John, Chuck and I had been chatting at the newlyweds' backyard reception when John turned and sauntered over to the punch bowl. The afternoon was muggy. Beads of perspiration trickled down from John's temples. My white rayon, long-sleeved, A-line dress was all wrong for such a sultry day, although the matching hat kept the intense sun from scorching the top of my head.

"Why don't you ditch that guy and marry me?" Chuck had said after taking a sip from his glass.

I squinted as I looked up at Chuck. With my hand shielding my eyes, I hoped to catch the expression on his face.

"Hey, your beau is coming back, see you," Chuck said as he sauntered away to join another group of guests.

The next time I saw Chuck was the following January, after John had broken off our one-month engagement.

16

My return

1969

There was no doubt as to where I wanted to work once I returned to Toronto. The Hospital for Sick Children had a vacancy in hematology. *Perfect.* I got a job as a secretary, taking the place of a woman who had left to become a stay-at-home mom. My position would be permanent—as permanent as anything ever was in my life.

The work at Sick Kids' was the best job I had ever had. Being the aunt of ten nieces and nephews, whom I loved and enjoyed being around, I found that working there gave me a sense of purpose. Although not a health care worker, I had direct contact with the children when they came to the office for their check-ups.

At the time, a number of children under my bosses' care had acute leukemia—a fast-growing, usually fatal, type of blood disorder. When their mothers brought them to the office, they would sit on the stiff brown leather sofa directly in front of my desk. As they waited for their appointment to see the Chief of Hematology, Dr. P.D. McClure, I would leave the work I was doing at my electric typewriter and speak to the mothers.

I felt a deep sense of compassion—a compassion that, many years later, would lead me into bereavement work. I could see the ache of each mother's heart and the sorrow for what was and what they knew was yet to come. Chronic listlessness seemed to accompany them with subsequent visits. It was as though they were going through the process of dying along with their child. In a sense, I believe they were.

I observed the look of death in these children: their emaciated, gaunt faces, with eyes sunken into circular sockets. The sickliest of children would be tucked securely against their mothers' chests, limbs resting limp and lifeless.

On his first appointment, a chubby little four-year-old, named Danny, came ambling into the office holding onto his mother's hand. Over the months, he regressed into total dependency: no longer able to walk, no longer able to hold his head up, no longer able to smile. As he sat on his mother's lap, his head drooped down toward his chest.

I recall the bone marrow aspiration in the lab down the hall. Through that narrow, dark corridor, Danny's screams pierced my eardrums and stabbed at my heart, forcing tears down my cheeks. A hymn I'd known all of my life would play in my mind, "When mothers of Salem, their children brought to Jesus...."[15]

Such torment penetrated my mind and put my own angst into clearer perspective. Compassion had previously eluded me, my lack of empathy essentially stemming from self-absorption. I saw myself as a flawed person—different from everyone else—never quite measuring up, and thinking, always thinking, I didn't fit in. This had stayed with me throughout adolescence and into adulthood—that old black crow that continued to tear away at my soul.

★ ★ ★ ★ ★

The strobe lights flickered on and off. I could see Chuck's face as we danced together—watched his body moving as we danced apart—to the music of the Fifth Dimension, "Let the sunshine in. Just open up your heart and let it shine on in."[16]

I felt the warmth of his open smile. The intermittent darkness hid his face, but still, I envisioned his deep dimpled cheeks, his tall stature.

Earlier that evening, the doorbell had rung. I was alone in the apartment I shared with my three roommates. I was on the phone with Dad. Mom made the initial call just to chat, but Dad had grabbed the phone from her hand.

"I'm dying, Claudia," he said.

"What are you talking about?" My anxiety escalated like a carnival strength-tester's puck shooting up to the bell.

Dad always seemed to have the ability to keep me anxious, despite the miles between us.

"Give me that phone, Claude!" I heard Mom say. "Don't pay any attention to him—he's having a bad day."

Mom didn't tell me Dad had been drinking, but clearly he had been. His words were garbled. He was talking crazy—just like his own father who used to tell Grandma and Aunt Olive he was going to kill himself.

"He's fine," Mom assured me, but it was too late. Worry and fear perched themselves, one upon each of my shoulders.

Is Mom hiding something from me? No, it's just Dad being Dad!

I found a Kleenex on the cherry wood coffee table beside the phone cradle and blotted my tears. Composing myself, I opened the door for my date.

He was strikingly handsome in his black-and-white plaid cotton pants and open-necked white, long-sleeved, cotton shirt.

"What's wrong?" asked Chuck

My eyes feel swollen. They're red, I know.

"I just got off the phone with my dad. He has an uncanny ability to upset me—said he was dying. He's been drinking."

The words tumbled from my mouth without forethought, before I realized my comments might bring questions from Chuck.

The thought jolted me. I turned my face away from him, fearful that I would begin to cry. Chuck touched my chin—it was a gentle touch, one that conveyed tenderness. I looked up at him.

"Your Dad…is he an alcoholic?"

"Why would you ask me that?" I grabbed each arm of the white cotton sweater I'd thrown over my shoulders and ran my moist hands down each sleeve.

"We've been dating long enough for me to pick up on the nuances in our conversations. I had a hunch."

I nodded. At that moment, I felt unfettered from the handcuffs of fear—accepted, not judged—maybe even loved, by the man I'd begun to love.

Enfolding me in his arms, he gave me a soothing squeeze, then said, "Let's go to the Electric Circus[17] and have some fun."

Chuck turned the doorknob with his right hand, firmly holding my own with his left. He guided me into the corridor and softly closed the door.

17

No longer alone

1969

By July 1969, Chuck and I were dating seriously. During that time, our conversation had led to the issue of faith and the importance of it in Chuck's own life. He had been raised in a Christian family and was the son of a pastor. At the time, his dad, Rev. Willem Loopstra, was minister of the Canadian Reformed Church in Hamilton, Ontario. He had received a call in 1951 to move to Canada from The Netherlands to pastor a church primarily composed of Dutch immigrants.

Along with his father, mother and three brothers, Klaas Mente (who later became known as Chuck) reached the shoreline of Halifax, Nova Scotia, when he was almost nine years old.

★ ★ ★ ★ ★

For too long, I'd neglected to find a place of worship in Toronto. Although I often accompanied my mother to church when I was home in Welland, my attendance had been as slack as a fishless fisherman's line. Loving the liturgy did not provide the impetus necessary to carry me through from Sunday to Sunday. The short homilies did not move me. Sleeping in was more appealing, despite the enjoyment I experienced at church as the minister led his flock through the familiar liturgy.

"I believe in God—yes—and in Jesus Christ," I said to Chuck, "but my attendance has been poor…in fact, it's been non-existent for a couple of years."

"You need to get back, then."

"I know."

On a clammy mid-August Sunday, I walked north from St. Clair subway station. Two seagulls flapped their wings and made ear-piercing, shrieking sounds a few yards above my head. I looked down at my watch and stepped up my pace. *Five more minutes to make the eleven o'clock service.* Taking in a deep breath, I sped up.

The day was oppressive. The muggy air immersed me in a mixture of smells: burnt hotdogs, mustard and beer. To my right, garbage from last night's street activity overflowed from a trash can. Even though I pinched my nose, I couldn't block out the stench. My thoughts turned to the last reunion at my brother-in-law's family cottage on Lake Erie. Hot dogs, hamburgers and beer had been the standard reunion fare. *Dad should never have gone.*

As I continued to rush, I could see Christ Church Anglican looming grand and imposing at Deer Park. The heavy wooden doors were open. I walked in. At my request, the greeter ushered me down the aisle to seat me near the front. Bowing my head before the altar, I took my place and kneeled to pray on the *prie-dieu.*

The organ played; the singing began. I turned and watched as the server carried the brass cross down the aisle. Behind him were two altar boys. The choir followed; the minister came next. I was engulfed in a feeling of reverential worship.

This is where I need to be. What took me so long to return?

The bulletin stated that Holy Communion would be administered at this service. I listened to the familiar words I'd once memorized for when the minister made preparations for the sacrament—he would chant the words from the Book of Common Prayer and the congregation would respond.

Therefore with Angels and Archangels,
   And with all the company of heaven,
We laud and magnify thy glorious Name;
   Evermore praising thee, and saying:
      "Holy, holy, holy, Lord God of hosts,

Heaven and earth are full of thy glory:
Glory be to thee, O Lord most High. Amen."[18]

Recollections of the Sundays spent in the girls' choir at Holy
Trinity Church in Welland quickly brought a familiar comfort.
The Anglican liturgy I was accustomed to during my choir days,
took me to—what I believed to be—the height of my faith in God.

★ ★ ★ ★ ★

As Chuck spoke to me about the importance of faith in his life,
despite the comfort provided by the Anglican Church, I wanted to
know more about Chuck's place of worship: How did it differ?
How was it similar?

In late August, on a canoe outing in Algonquin Park, as I listened to the droplets drip from my paddle into the water, I looked
across at Chuck and said, "I would like to go to church with you
tomorrow, okay?"

He stopped paddling, leaned forward and nodded, "Yes…yes, I
would like that very much." Chuck enthusiastically picked up his
paddle and starting paddling hard.

"Hey—wait—let me catch up—we're going in circles. I'm getting dizzy!"

I was no match for his energy level.

"It takes thirty minutes to drive to the church," Chuck said as he
dropped me off at my apartment later that evening. "I'll pick you
up at 9:30 sharp!" He gave me a quick kiss and left.

★ ★ ★ ★ ★

The one-storey, white clapboard church on Centre Street in
North Toronto was packed. The congregation had outgrown this
historic church and a new church was being built nearby. Chuck
escorted me to the front where we squeezed into the second row—
barely enough room for the two of us. A dark-haired, teenage boy
with soft, light-coloured fuzz over his upper lip, looked up at me,
smiled and shifted over.

Sweet, mannerly—I feel welcomed.

Dressed in a black clerical gown, with a white shirt and red tie visible above the gown's scooped neckline, the minister entered the sanctuary through a side door at the front of the church. A portly man, dressed in a dark suit, followed. Reverend Kouwenhoven turned toward the man. They both nodded and shook hands as though they had just settled a disagreement. *Odd.*

Where's the server who carries the cross? The altar boys...followed by the choir, followed by the minister?

Chuck took my hand. We stood up together. The pews creaked as the congregation rose.

The minister raised his hands as though he was about to be arrested. My inclination was to turn around. *Anything is possible in Toronto.*

"Our help is in the name of the Lord, who made heaven and earth."

Where's the choir? They must have a choir.

While Chuck thumbed his way through the *Book of Praise*, I began thinking about the Sunday morning communion services of my junior girls' choir days. We would sit in the pews at the front of the church behind the elevated pulpit. The congregation would respond to each of the Ten Commandments as the minister recited them. We knelt while we rested our hands on the top of the pew in front of us.

"And God spoke these words, and said; I am the Lord thy God; Thou shalt have none other gods but me."

"Lord, have mercy upon us, and incline our hearts to keep this law,"[19] responded the congregation...and on through the remainder of the Ten Commandments. On the tenth, the people murmured, "Lord, have mercy upon us, and write all these laws in our hearts, we beseech thee." All of this had been spoken while the congregation remained kneeling.

Here, at Bethel Canadian Reformed Church, after the salutation, the congregation continued to stand.

Chuck held the *Book of Praise* open to the hymn listed on the black hymn board. The congregation joined in as the pipe organ began to play the prelude

I love the Lord, the fount of life and grace;
He heard my voice, my cry and supplication,

Inclined His ear, gave strength and consolation
In life, in death, my heart will seek his face.

The robust voices of the congregation sang out with zest. The piece was unfamiliar to me but, with my ear for music, I joined in with ease.

I had never experienced a congregation singing with such whole-hearted enthusiasm.

I cried to Him, "Oh, I beseech Thee, LORD,
   Preserve my Life and prove Thyself my Saviour!"
The LORD is just and He shows grace and favour;
   In boundless mercy He fulfils His word."[20]

The order of service continued with a reading from Exodus 20:2–17 (the Ten Commandments). No response was expected from the congregation. I crossed and uncrossed my legs.

I looked down at the bulletin—a hymn. Chuck took my hand again as we sang together. This time, we were told to remain seated.

If you but let the Father guide you.
   Relying on His faithfulness.
He will be evermore beside you
   In all your sorrow and distress.
He who on God Most High depends
   Builds not his house on shifting sands.[21]

Father—guide me? Not my father. He caused all of my misery. Undependable, too. Talk about building a house on shifting sands!

The reading of God's Word came next—Scripture that related to the sermon—followed by the minister leading the congregation in prayer. *Mmm, the offering collection is next.* I crossed my legs, pulling at the hem of my cotton, lime-green mini-dress. I shifted in my seat. Chuck put his arm around my shoulder and drew me near. Oh, such a public display of affection! The people behind will clearly see this.

I looked at the bulletin—another hymn after the offering collection. None were familiar to me, yet I joined in with eagerness as the congregation lifted their voices, singing praises to God. Although his voice broke occasionally, the teen to my left sang with gusto.

As the minister was about to begin his sermon, I felt a tap on my left arm. I turned toward the teen. Clenched in his hand was a roll of peppermints. *Eating candy in church—doesn't that border on sacrilege?* Chuck gave me a nudge—interpreted by me as "Take one." I took a candy from the open end of the package, hesitated for a couple of seconds, then, quickly popped it into my mouth. "Thanks," I whispered, as a dribble of drool escaped from the corner of my mouth. I felt my face blanch. The boy reached over my lap and offered a mint to Chuck, who nodded in silent appreciation. My teenaged friend licked the white peppermint and popped it into his mouth.

"Kleenex," I murmured to Chuck. Into his pant pocket, went his hand. He passed me a jumbo-sized tissue. *He is so not subtle!* I sat still for a few seconds until the minister began his sermon. Feigning an adjustment to the strap of my sandal, I bent toward the floor. While down there, I quickly dabbed my mouth. A clear spot appeared on the lower part of my dress. I rapidly sat erect and looked ahead.

Following the sermon, Rev. Kouwenhoven prayed. We sang the closing song; the minister's hands took flight again as he recited the benediction from 2 Corinthians 13:14 (NIV): "The grace of the Lord Jesus Christ and the love of God and the fellowship of the Holy Spirit be with you all." "Amen."

After the service, a number of people came up to us. Chuck introduced me as his girlfriend. Eyebrows were raised; faces lit up with interest. Chuck was poked in the ribs a couple of times. It was all too embarrassing and ridiculously obvious. *Ah, the eligible bachelor may be settling down.*

Despite the vast differences in the way the Reformed service had been conducted, from our discussions, I knew the tenets of the faith were basically the same. I also felt welcomed. I loved how the people were fully engaged in the singing of the hymns. It was something I'd not experienced in the Anglican Church.

"I have a lot of questions for you," I said, as we drove away from the church in Chuck's navy blue Alfa Romeo. "What's with the candy, by the way?"

"In the old days, when the sermons were long, it prevented people from falling asleep. The women used to carry a roll of peppermints in their purses. Husbands seemed more inclined to nod off. The tradition stuck. Rather nice, don't you think?"

"I suppose if you have coffee breath. It doesn't seem respectful to me."

"You *did* take one, though."

"M-m-m, so I did."

"I have a suggestion for you. Evening catechism classes are beginning in September. If you want to learn more about our church, why don't you take the classes? I'll set it up for you."

"Does that mean I would be taking classes with thirteen-year-olds? I already did catechism classes and was confirmed the year I turned thirteen."

"It would be a brush-up course. The young people in our church don't begin taking catechism classes until they're in high school. They usually finish after four years. We refer to confirmation as "profession of faith." Anyway, I'll get in touch with the minister and talk to him about it. Do you want me to?"

"Okay. I'll leave my questions for the teacher."

★ ★ ★ ★ ★

Brown, crisp October leaves swirled around our feet as Chuck reached for the door handle of the Jolly Miller Tavern. The whistling wind ushered us into the pub of this nineteenth-century red brick, three-storey structure at the bottom of a slope in Hoggs Hollow.

It was Tuesday evening. Chuck had just picked me up from catechism class at the church. He'd done this since I began the classes in mid-September. Rev. Kouwenhoven had died of a heart attack shortly after I attended my first service at Bethel. The congregation felt bereft over the loss of this well-loved man. A theology student named Menno Werkman had been brought in to teach me and one other young woman from the church. After our drinks had been placed before us by the waiter, Chuck asked, "If we were to get married, would you prefer to go to Europe in January or March?" His impish grin left no doubt as to what he was intending to elicit from me with this cockeyed approach.

"Huh?" I stared back at him. It was the first time the "M" word had been mentioned although, in the summer, he had declared his love for me. Well, he somehow manipulated me into telling him first.

He's going to ask me properly...none of this fishing around in his oblique way.

Chuck said nothing. He waited.

I took a sip of my beer, swallowed and said, "January!"

My pulse began to race.

"Let's make it March. The Keukenhof Flower Exhibition will be on then."

18

Challenges

1970

The car rolled to a stop in a park near our home in Rosedale. A kaleidoscope of warm, vibrant colours surrounded us. Moist leaves glistened as the sun filtered through the near-barren branches of the tall maple trees. Chuck turned off the ignition. All was quiet. I closed my eyes and leaned against the head rest.

We were on our way to a 4:30 p.m. church service, when I burst into tears. Chuck made an abrupt U-turn and drove into the park.

The reality was I came into my 1970 marriage with one suitcase full of clothes, one suitcase full of debts and a trunkload full of insecurities. I had naively believed that marrying the man I loved would obliterate all things holding me captive to my past.

"What's wrong with you?" asked Chuck. "You seem to be unhappy lately."

"I feel miserable. I don't want to do anything; I don't want to go anywhere."

I unfastened my seatbelt and began to undo the buttons of my cocoa-coloured wool coat.

"You are happy about having the baby, aren't you?" Chuck queried. His thick, blonde eyebrows became a crumpled cluster of worry.

"I am—of course—it's Dad, again. It's always him."

I paused and thought about the conversation I had with Craig shortly after Father's Day—how hurt and rebuffed Dad made my teenage brother feel.

"What about your dad?" asked Chuck.

"For Father's Day, Craig made Dad a replica of the *Titanic*. He told me he'd spent a lot of time on it. Apparently, Dad became angry with him over some minor incident—according to Craig—and told him to take his gift back—he didn't want anything from him. Craig wouldn't take it back. The next day, when Craig opened his bedroom door, there sat the replica."

"But, Father's Day was in June. This is October. Why is this upsetting you now?" Chuck asked while reaching for my hand. "And, why didn't you tell me before this?"

"I pushed it away. I don't like to dwell on the hurtful things Dad does."

Chuck was an attentive listener; never judgemental, rarely critical.

"You need to talk about what bothers you. Look! Look at you... you're so distraught."

I grabbed the tissue Chuck handed to me. With it, I gave my nose a hardy blow.

Why does my father's behaviour continue to have such a hold on me?

★ ★ ★ ★ ★

Dr. Ravinsky, my obstetrician, a little man with grey, frizzy hair atop his receding hairline, sat in his armchair with elbows bowed outward. His clenched fists supported his double chin. His index fingers were crossed and pressed into his jaw.

He reached over his desk to hand me a white business card with the name, address and phone number of a psychiatrist. It had surprised me when he mentioned I should consider getting some professional help.

How transparent am I?

I had no insight into his tip-off about me. I only knew I was relieved when he gave me the referral.

A month later, I sat in Dr. Marguelies' office at my third appointment. He asked me a question that opened a floodgate of tears. I wept as I related the story about Dad and how he had hurt Craig. Re-opening a wound that I considered healed, I cried like a

My brother Craig with the model of the Titanic *he made for Dad.*

five-year-old who had just fallen off her bike.

I moved on to the story about the wristwatch Dad gave me for my thirteenth birthday; the way I felt about how he had wounded Mom. I reached for the Kleenex box sitting on top of Dr. Marguelies's desk. No doubt, the expensive-looking brass tissue holder had a permanent home on his desk, close to the patient's chair.

One story about my life with Dad flowed into the next—the next and the next. Dr. Marguelies sat in silence as I continued to talk and cry hysterically. I heaved and sobbed.

"The hour is up, now, Claudia. Shall we book your next appointment?"

"Not sure yet. I'll call you," I snivelled.

I knew I needed some time to recover from my conflicting feelings about whether or not this had been helpful for me. A sensation of numbness crept over my body.

That was exhausting!

Walking out into the cool, damp November air, heading for the University Street subway, I looked toward the cloudless sky and sighed. Eventually, my walk turned into a brisk jog. Oh, how I wanted Chuck to hold me at that very moment. Looking down at my watch, I realized it would be three hours before he finished work and another forty-five minutes before he would walk through our front door.

By the time I reached home, thirty minutes later, I began to experience a sense of well-being. It spurred me into tackling a job I'd put off for longer than I cared to consider.

Into the fridge I went. I pulled out barely identifiable food items that looked as though they could have grown legs and jumped out of the refrigerator on their own. *Whew, that musty, earthy smell— disgusting!* I slapped my hand over my mouth and nose and headed for our tiny, mauve-coloured bathroom. Morning sickness had plagued me since the beginning of my pregnancy but usually, by midday, I could tolerate odours.

I will not be deterred from the job at hand!

After I finished throwing out most of the contents of the refrigerator, I removed the remains and cleaned each shelf with warm water and two squirts of dish detergent. I made up a bicarbonate of soda paste—just like Mom—to clean the gooey areas. My accomplishment made me proud. By the time Chuck reached home, dinner was waiting for him.

"I smell my mother's chicken recipe. You sprinkled it with nutmeg?" I nodded. "Let me guess: apple sauce, glazed beets and mashed potatoes—I love glazed beets." When I turned to face Chuck, he wrapped his arms around me as I nuzzled into his warmth.

"How did your appointment go?" he asked, still holding me close.

"I've never cried so hard. I wanted to run from his office and never go back."

"You *are* going back, though."

"Hmmm, maybe not."

Chuck dropped his arms, shifted his weight and stood still in expectation of further discussion.

"Dinner's ready. We'll talk about it...over dinner."

Although counselling had been helpful, I continued to be emotionally distant from my father for another fifteen years.

Our wedding day, March 5, 1970, with Mom and Dad.

19

The early years

1971–1975
I was enraptured by my easy-going baby born on April 24, 1971.
Melinda made motherhood a gratifying and pleasurable experience.

In 1973, Chuck arranged to have the house at 56 Oakland
Avenue appraised. Mom and Dad were getting by on their old age
pensions, but the house needed significant repairs. My parents
did not have the money for the much-needed renovations.

Mom had expressed her concern over the possibility of being
forced to sell the house. After having it appraised, Chuck purchased it from Mom and Dad at market value. He paid off the
remainder of the mortgage. The difference between the mortgage
and the appraised value was put into a non-interest-bearing trust
fund for my parents, a fund not to be accessed until they moved
out of the house. During this time, they lived rent-free.

Chuck had gone ahead with the renovations. Every window was
replaced since the frames were beginning to rot. New wiring was
installed; the upstairs bathroom was re-done as well as the kitchen.
White aluminum siding replaced the clapboard exterior.

Mom and Dad were filled with gratitude at Chuck's benevolence.
God, you gave to me a kind and generous husband.

On April 8, 1975, Cameron was born, adding to my fulfillment.
My life had taken a dramatic turn with marriage and children.
Never before had I felt so secure and loved.

★ ★ ★ ★ ★

"Debbie's in the hospital, again." Dad stood on the bottom step of the worn oak stairs leading to the second floor when Mom gave him the news.

It was January 1977, when a deadly blizzard hit southern Ontario. During the snowstorm, my cousin Barbara's twelve-year-old daughter, Debbie, had been rushed to the hospital. She had a connective tissue disorder that affected her muscles. It also left her with a weakened immune system. As a result, Debbie had developed a severe case of pneumonia.

"That poor kid," said Dad, after Mom told him.

He turned and glanced out the window at the ice daggers hanging from the arbour's wooden frame. This latest development gave my father pause to focus on someone else's suffering. As often happened, a bout of depression had rendered Dad incapable of leaving his room for a number of days. Mom brought his meals upstairs, leaving his tray in front of his closed door. Hours later, she collected the tray, at times untouched, returning it to the kitchen.

Mom covered her mouth as she looked my father up and down. A bristly growth of stubble covered his cheeks and chin. The shirt he wore was heavily soiled with food. One frayed maroon-striped suspender drooped below the waist of his faded brown trousers. He reeked of perspiration.

The following day, my father shovelled the snow from the driveway, cleaned off his mint-green Pontiac and drove away. He returned an hour later with a three-foot, ten-inch white box. Inside was a life-sized doll with long brown curly hair. She had blue eyes that opened and closed. Her beautiful face had the flawlessness of the very young. She couldn't walk like the dolls I once loved to play with, but she was perfect for a young girl who was confined to a hospital bed.

Debbie's new doll was splendidly attired in a pink satin gown with wrist-length sleeves and a neckline trimmed in cream-coloured lace. Her feet's clear plastic shoes were attached to a stand. I could visualize her as a celestial being who would watch over Debbie during the winter's long, dark nights.

Dad, in all of his complexity, was an enigma. Yet, this kind, compassionate act demonstrated the tenderness of a man with a heart for those who suffered—as doubtless, he did, in ways we couldn't understand.

* * * * *

Throughout the years, my father continued to have his binges— not that Mom talked about it. On this matter, unless my visit came at an inopportune time, and a simple statement of fact was needed, she remained mute. Every so often, I was caught off guard when I visited. By the grace of God, Cameron and Melinda were spared any exposure to the effects of their grandfather's over-indulgences.

My own journal entries, however, disclosed the times when I witnessed the results of his intemperance.

Friday, September 2, 1977
Stayed at Shirley and [husband] *Bob's until 10:30 p.m. Chuck dropped me off at Mom and Dad's. He went back to our trailer* [at Sherkston]. *I have to go to the hairdresser with Mom in the morning. Dad's bombed.*

"Your Dad's been drinking. He's in bed," Mom said as she greeted me with a hug. It was the evening before Carl's oldest daughter's wedding.

"Oh, brother!"

I threw up my hands. There was nothing more to say.

Mom led the way into the kitchen. She offered me a cup of tea. We chatted until the white-and-pink flowered china pot was emptied. Up to the second floor we tiptoed. As I entered the bathroom, I was overcome by a pungent, noxious stench—a combination of urine and putrid unidentifiable foulness. Dad coughed and heaved in his bedroom. A dresser drawer banged loudly.

Gotta get into my bedroom before he comes out of his!

I rushed out of the bathroom and into the room I was to share with my mother. Despite the near-confrontation, sleep came quickly. It had been an exhausting day.

Saturday, September 3, 1977
Mom had one big mess to clean up in Dad's room. He was soaked
with beer. When she went in at 6 a.m., he was sitting on the floor
in front of the TV with beer bottles all over the place. Mom and I
went to the hairdresser's at 9:30. Beautiful day. Needless to say,
Dad didn't go to Karen's wedding.

Wouldn't you know? Dad got drunk before my wedding, too. No
surprises here.
Although there had been the acute reality of Dad's presence
during my short stay, he was like a phantom—skulking about
without appearing.

* * * * *

Sunday, October 2, 1977
Went to church. Not crazy about the new minister. He preached for
over an hour. Irritated me. I could have sucked on an entire roll of
peppermints today!

At that point, I had been tuning out the sermons for a number
of months. My faith had weakened. I kept it to myself and continued to go to church with my family.

* * * * *

Sunday, October 16, 1977
Got up at 8:50. Had to babysit at church. As it turned out there
was an extra teenager downstairs so I went to the service. Had
lunch at home. Went to Craig's for supper. Mom and Trish were
there. We took the kids. Craig made lasagna and broccoli, with
homemade apple pie for dessert. It was good. We watched some
movies. The kids watched movies in the bedroom for a while. Mom
left at 5:45 to catch the bus [from Toronto] *at 6. Chuck took her*
to the station.

* * * * *

When the movie—about a gay couple—came to an end, the moderate temperature in the room took a nose-dive. My skin began to tingle. I folded my arms across my chest, and rubbed my arms vigorously with my palms. The sweet aftertaste of apple pie was gone, my mouth dust-dry.

"Are you trying to tell us," asked Chuck, "that you're gay, Craig?"

Craig solemnly nodded his head; then, looked directly at Chuck. I suppose he knew what kind of response he'd get from his two outspoken sisters.

"Oh, no!" Trisha blurted out. Trisha—who had come back to Ontario and settled in Burlington with her four children. Trisha—whose husband had left her and married his partner in infidelity.

"Good thing Mom's not here." I said. "She'd have a stroke!"

I gazed over at the veneer wooden cabinet where Craig had placed the rejected replica of the *Titanic* he had once built for Dad.

We grew as quiet as a small group of veterans acknowledging two minutes' silence on Remembrance Day.

Chuck spoke up, his voice uncharacteristically soft, "You know Craig, we don't agree with the homosexual lifestyle, but you're our brother—you're family. We care about you."

Craig looked over at Trisha and me. I unfolded my legs from the couch and reached down for my black leather pumps. I slid my feet into each shoe. Trish remained seated—her hand resting on the arm of the chair.

I got up, walked over to Craig and gave him a hug. His arms dangled by his side.

"Nothing is going to change between us, Craig. It won't!"

I had no idea how wrong I was.

20

A grandmother's and an uncle's love

1970s

Mom had continued to work past retirement age, but once she retired, she finally had time to enjoy her grandchildren.

"I love you, Grandma," said Melinda one day as Mom stood at her kitchen counter packing up our lunch to take to Crystal Beach. We visited the amusement park with my mother every summer until my children became teenagers.

Mom's hands stopped working the zipper on the red vinyl cooler with the white plastic piping. She patted my seven-year-old daughter's head and said, "I love you too, Honey."

I've never heard her say that before. And, "Honey"—not a word Mom used.

I was pleased.

When Craig eventually told Mom he was gay, she was taken aback. All the family were present when he made his announcement. Mom stared down at the floor and said, "Craig, you'll never have children." Her voice broke as she spoke.

It was then I realized we, as Mom's children, were the source of her fulfillment and any happiness she experienced. It had kept her going.

Dad liked children. For the most part, he had been attentive to Melinda and Cameron when they were young tykes. He drew cartoons, contorted his whiskered face until he made the children laugh hysterically and used old socks to make hand puppets. Once they grew older, he became less interested. It was a familiar pattern, experienced by my siblings and me.

In later years, Dad became somewhat of a recluse. Even though he was always invited to our home along with Mom, he rarely came. Nor did he go with us to Crystal Beach. I didn't care, and the children never inquired.

* * * * *

My youngest brother and I became closer when he became an adult. Beginning in his twenties, we made arrangements to see one another frequently.

By the early 1970s, Craig moved away from Welland to Toronto. He worked at Black's and then at a small Toronto bookstore, continuing to work there after he started his studies in film at York University. His interest in the film industry seemed to stimulate a desire to entertain his twelve nieces and nephews. With every visit to our home, he brought his cache of rented movies. He would set up his projector in our family room and then sit down with the children snuggled in close to him eating popcorn.

In the late 1970s, Craig would often take Melinda and Cameron for a weekend visit at his downtown apartment. They took trips to the movie theatres, ate endless boxes of popcorn and took numerous subway rides. They always returned home full of excitement as they filled Chuck and me in on "the best time!"

After Craig completed his third year at York, he was hired by CBC. He made new friends, and we all saw less of him.

21

Hard-hearted

Be kind and compassionate to one another, forgiving each other, just as in Christ God forgave you (Ephesians 4:32, NIV).

Early 80s

"You have no compassion," said Mom after she listened to my complaints about my father's behaviour.

Trisha, Shirley, Mom, Dad and I were on a two-week vacation in Florida together. It was the early 80s, and at the time, Chuck and I owned a condominium on Longboat Key near Sarasota, Florida.

"Compassion, Mom? Dad's been drinking on and off since last week. He sat on the baggage carousel at the airport, remember? If it hadn't been for one of the ground employees lifting him off, he'd still be going around with the luggage!"

I wanted to ask Mom why she let Dad order a drink on the plane, but the answer was obvious: "He would have made a scene."

"Just now, Mom, when I took his tea into the bedroom, he was teetering on the edge of the bed with Melinda's bathing cap sitting on the top of his head. When I asked him 'why' he had the cap on, he smiled his silly Clem Kadiddlehopper[22] smile and said he was going swimming. He doesn't even *know* how to swim! Dad's drinking again. He smells like a fermented grape—it sets my teeth on edge. How can I have compassion?"

It no doubt embarrassed Mom to know Dad was getting into

Chuck's liquor. I hid it in the closet next to our en suite bathroom when we arrived. It must have happened during our afternoon dips in the pool. I pictured Dad skulking around the house like a mouse in search of a piece of cheese.

Mom shook her head and stared me down until I looked away. She continued peeling the potatoes for dinner. I took a plastic bag of green beans out of the fridge and gently put three handfuls of beans into the pot. I knew I bruised Mom with my words, but I couldn't apologize. My raw feelings of anger toward Dad ran deep. *It's just like him to spoil everyone's vacation—especially Mom's.*

Despite all my father's mental and physical challenges, compassion for him continued to elude me. At that point, I knew nothing of God's requirement to show compassion or love toward someone who caused such deep-seated emotional pain.

"Excuse me, Mom, I need to rinse these," I said softly. She moved over but kept her eyes riveted on the potatoes. In silence, we prepared the meal together.

★ ★ ★ ★ ★

There had been a time—according to Dad but not verified by Mom—when he daily took thirty-six 222 tablets for his arthritis-riddled back. Possibly the numbers were exaggerated by Dad, but his intermittent bizarre behaviour, in addition to his stomach pain, precipitated Mom's insistence on him visiting his doctor.

Dad was asked the usual questions, including what medications he was taking. After the doctor examined my father and had him x-rayed, they discovered something had destroyed half of Dad's stomach. An operation followed.

Soon after, Dad's family doctor referred him to a psychiatrist. My father went on anti-depressants and, although the medication seemed to lessen his depression, he still exhibited unpredictable behaviour.

It wasn't determined whether the 222s (with codeine) caused Dad's whacky behaviour—or if it was the alcohol. Just as Dad quit smoking cigarettes following his doctor's challenge to give them up, he later quit drinking altogether.

$$22$$

The Philp curse

"…for I, the LORD your God, am a jealous God, punishing the children for the sin of the parents to the third and fourth generation of those who hate me, but showing love to a thousand generations of those who love me and keep my commandments" Exodus 20:5–6 (NIV).

1980s

After Mom retired, I often visited my parents for the day in Welland. I would leave in the morning after Melinda and Cameron got on the school bus, and return before they got home in the late afternoon.

On one such day, Mom was baking a lemon cake in the kitchen, adjacent to the living room, while Dad and I sat at the dining room table drinking our tea.

At one point, Dad turned and faced me. He sucked in his upper lip. Then, he sighed and began tapping his nicotine-stained fingers on the table. He shook his head back and forth as he looked over at the 16" x 20" sepia-toned portrait of Grandpa Philp, wearing his fedora hat, camel-hair coat and an unmistakable sneer. The picture hung on the dining room wall next to the walnut china cabinet.

"One day, I got a call from Mother," began Dad. "She was crying. She told me Dad had gone down the cellar to hang himself, so I left the dinner table and rushed over to the house. Mother and Olive were sitting in the living room huddled together on the chesterfield, bawling into their hankies. I went through to the kitchen and stood by the basement door for a few seconds. I could hear the old man's voice. When I opened the door and went down the steps, I found him sitting on a paint can singing, 'When Irish Eyes are Smiling.' It likely pleased him to upset the two of them. He got pleasure watching his family stew. He harped on killing himself until he finally ended up in the loony bin."

I didn't know Grandpa Philp very well, but many stories had circulated about him. Grandpa had remained in an institution until his death as the result of a heart attack in July 1958.

Hmmm, I remember the summer when I was about five years old. My cousin Stewart and I had our picture taken with Grandpa on the grey-painted steps in front of his house. He held each one of us on a separate knee. After the photo was taken, Grandpa stood up, reached into his pant pocket and handed Stewart a dime. I stood and watched—waiting. Nothing. Mean...he had a real mean streak. That's what I remember about him.

My father continued, "And when Leo was alive—before Dad started saying he was going to kill himself...."

"Your brother had tuberculosis, right?"

"Yeah...he only lived to be twenty-one—not long enough to meet a girl and get married. Did I tell you what happened the day before he died?" Dad asked, as he shifted in his chair, folded his arms and leaned on the table.

Just then, Mom came into the dining room from the kitchen. She had finished putting her cake into the oven. It was the cake she would be taking to Shirley's that afternoon.

Mom appeared tired. Her short-cropped curly hair, feathered with grey streaks, needed combing. She was beginning to resemble her own mother, with a good number of wrinkles surrounding her mouth. Still, her blue eyes remained acutely clear.

Mom frowned as she stood wiping her hands on her orange-and-white-checked, terry apron.

How many times has Mom heard this story—and more—about the father-in-law that she disliked?

"The cake is in the oven. I'm going upstairs to change before we go out to visit Shirley," she said.

Mom walked through the dining room's double doors, passing through the living room into the hall. I could hear the sweeping of her slippers as she slowly climbed the staircase to the second floor.

I breathed in the aroma of Mom's cake—a simple recipe with a drizzle of lemon juice mixed with icing sugar for the topping. Although made from a mix, the family thought of it as Mom's signature recipe—the type of icing being her own idea. Whenever I caught a whiff of my mother's lemon cake, I inhaled the fragrant memories of Wednesday afternoons, when she would be home from work: washing, waxing the floors and making a delectable dinner that appealed to this child's palete. Her lip-smacking lemon cake was often served at the end of the meal.

Dad waited until the sound of Mom's shuffling faded.

He cleared his throat. "The day before Leo died, your grandmother got a phone call from the sanatorium. The hospital was in St. Catharines—the closest one to Welland. It used to take about an hour to drive there. Leo knew he was dying. He wanted Mother to go and be with him. Dad wouldn't drive her there. She asked him for the money to take the train, but he wouldn't even give her that."

He paused. "Leo died alone."

"That's cruel," I said. "Wouldn't Grandpa want to see his own son before he died? Wouldn't he want to take Grandma? I don't understand, Dad. It sounds so heartless. Do you have any idea why?"

"Because he was a mean bugger. He only cared about himself."

Dad turned to face me. His distinctive square jawline tensed. He tapped his fingers on the table, again.

My father looked up at the photo hanging on the wall opposite to Grandpa's, next to the window.

Leo and Dad bore a strong resemblance to one another—the square jaw, the lock of black hair with the wave falling over the right side of the forehead. Both Dad and Leo had bushy eyebrows that arched over their eyes, then continued in a straight line above the bridge of their nose.

My father looked away from Leo's portrait. He began stirring his tepid tea. "Your mother used to work for Dad—back when we were first married. She was at her desk working on his books one

Friday afternoon when she noticed Dad overcharged his customer for the paint he sold him.

"He told your mother he watered down the paint, too. 'Real pleased with himself,' she told me. Your mother closed up the books, right then, got up from her chair and never went back to work for him again. He was such a crook!"

Throughout the years, Dad continued to tell me a story here and a story there about his father. Maybe, he could only do this in small doses because of the feelings it brought up. I sensed things were always uncertain with Grandpa—much the way I experienced life with Dad.

* * * * *

"Hello, Birdie," Mom greeted her neighbour. "C'mon in and have a cup of tea. Claudia's here."

Along with her husband, Orval, Birdie Gonyou, my brother Carl's mother-in-law, lived across the street from my parents' house. A friendly, chatty woman, Mrs. Gonyou occasionally popped by for a visit with Mom.

"No, I can't stay, Dora...but, say, do you know where Claude is?"

"He's upstairs lying down. His back's been bothering him more than usual. Why?"

"I think you need to get upstairs. He's on the roof—in his housecoat. Umm...he's not wearing anything under his housecoat. When I was out on my veranda talking to Mrs. Batterton, I could see him."

Mom blanched.

"Thank you, Birdie."

My mother said a quick "good-bye," closed the door, and we headed for the upstairs bedroom at the front of the house. The door to the first level roof was open. A few dry, brown leaves had blown onto the hardwood floor.

"Come in here right now, Claude!"

Dad obediently turned around and did what he was told.

"What do you think you're doing out there?" Mom demanded.

"Cleaning the leaves off the roof."

"With your bare hands?"

"Yar."

"Go to your room and get dressed. Birdie could see you from her house—and get some underwear on!"

* * * * *

As Dad got older, he became more dependent upon Mom. She would dole out his pills, keep tabs on his bathing habits and make sure he changed his clothes frequently.

I had never seen anyone perspire like my father. It was as though he was in a perpetual state of angst.

Mom would tell him what to do, and he would follow her instructions. She would have him wash his underarms every day, slather him with deodorant and tell him to go lie down with his arms stretched above his head until she deemed his deodorant sufficiently dry.

The first time I witnessed this ritual was on one of my visits to Welland. When I walked into the living room, Dad was lying on the couch, as still as a corpse, with bare arms extended above his head. I stood on the furnace grate watching the scene before me, bewildered as to what was going on.

"Can I put my arms down now, Dora?" Dad asked. He shifted his body and winced. I could see he was uncomfortable. Still, he kept his arms up until Mom spoke.

"Get off the couch and go put your shirt on."

23

Glow, little glow-worm

"I tell you the truth, no one can see the kingdom of God unless he is born again" (John 3:3).

In the summer of 1981, shortly before noon one day, the bus finally pulled into the parking lot of the Baptist church in Willowdale—a half-hour late. Melinda was one of the first to descend the steps. Her chin-length brown hair appeared a shade lighter than it was two weeks before; her bangs were highlighted with touches of blond. Melinda's tanned legs and arms reminded me of something her Dutch Grandma Loopstra used to say to anyone with a tan, "You're as brown as *en burry!*"

This was the first year my ten-year-old daughter had been away from home. On the recommendation of a lady who attended our church, I had signed her up to attend Beacon Bible Camp.

Melinda vaulted toward me. My arms encircled her small-framed body. I released my hold, stood back and looked at her as I rested my hands on her shoulders.

"You don't need to tell me—I can see by looking at you that you had a good time. You shine as bright as a glow-worm."

After picking up her blue duffel bag, we walked hand-in-hand toward the parking lot behind the church where I had left the car.

Just as I was about to open the trunk, Melinda released my hand, looked up at me and said, "Mommy, have you accepted Jesus Christ as your personal Saviour?"

What—where's this coming from?

Her question shook me from the pleasure I was feeling at her return.

I bristled.

"What are you talking about?"

Why on earth is she asking such a question? I've always gone to church with the family. I believe in God...a personal relationship with Jesus?

Before allowing Melinda to answer, I said, "It's none of your business."

"I'm going to tell Daddy," she said as she went around to the side of the car, opened the door and slid into the front seat.

I slammed down the trunk, walked to the driver's side of the car, paused, opened the door, sat down and wrenched on the ignition.

"Go ahead, tell Daddy. What's there to tell?"

I'm a God-fearing Christian. How dare Melinda question it? She's my daughter and only ten years old!

We drove home that day in silence. Melinda continued to stare out the window, saying nothing. I was too angry to discuss her camp experience, and I assumed she knew why.

What's the matter with me, anyway? I feel like Melinda is the mother checking up on her daughter. I'm acting more like the ten-year-old. A personal relationship with Jesus? What's that all about? Sounds as though Beacon is a "holy-roller" camp. Maybe, she shouldn't go there again.

Melinda didn't tell her father about our conversation. She kept it to herself. Maybe, she learned from my response, certain topics were, after all, off-limits for discussion. My reaction to her query, no doubt, left her confused. The subject wasn't broached again.

★ ★ ★ ★ ★

The alarm went off at 8:00 a.m. Chuck—a morning person—turned it off, plunked his feet on to the floor and proceeded to move briskly toward the bedroom door. It was Chuck's habit to do things quickly and efficiently.

I pulled the bedsheets under my chin as I rolled over from my left side to my right. The warmth of my blanket embraced me. I wasn't about to get up anytime soon.

"I'm not going to church with you this morning," I said. "I'm going to the gym."

He turned around just as he reached the door.

"You are *what?*"

Chuck walked back and looked down at me.

"You heard me right—I'm not going to church. I don't belong at Bethel. I want to look elsewhere. I'm not being fed."

"Out of the blue—just like that," was his only response.

When he left the bedroom, he closed the door behind him. I heard him climbing the steps to the second floor. Soon, Cameron and Melinda came bounding down the stairs. I could hear them pull the chairs out from our kitchen table. Chuck, no doubt, had their cereal poured into bowls.

No other sounds could be heard—I fell asleep. When Chuck returned to our bedroom to get dressed, I got up and went over to him.

"I'm sorry," I said. "I just need some time to sort things out."

"We're going to be late. I've got to get going."

He kissed me on the cheek, called the children and left for church. *Poor Chuck! He must be confused. He won't know what's going on. Am I rebelling against the ultra-conservative nature of the Canadian Reformed Church—the church in which he grew up? Am I rebelling against the fundamentals of the faith? Why doesn't he say something?*

How can I explain what is going on inside? I just feel so empty. I have everything going for me: a loving family, a good husband. I have been well-provided for. I should be blissfully happy. Yet, I feel miserable. It has to be the church!

Melinda's words continued to follow me. Mentally, I kept running, but the faster I ran, the louder the clamour of their persistent pursuit.

"Mom, have you accepted Jesus Christ as your personal Saviour?"

No, I have not!

24

Confused

"Sir," the [Samaritan] woman said, "you have nothing to draw with and the well is deep. Where can you get this living water?" Jesus answered, "Everyone who drinks this water will be thirsty again, but whoever drinks the water I give them will never thirst. Indeed, the water I give them will become in them a spring of water welling up to eternal life" (John 4:11,13–14, NIV).

1981
Six-year-old Cameron was standing with the refrigerator door open as I walked into the kitchen and tapped him on the shoulder. His eyes were scrunched together as he turned around.

"I know who you are—you're the bogeyman!" he chirped. His eyes popped open.

"I knew it was you, Mommy, cuz I heard you hummin' when you came down the hall."

Cameron's eyebrows lifted above his large, clear blue eyes. I bent over and kissed the top of his head. He had flaxen-coloured hair like his Dad—although, his eyes and eyebrows were the shape of my father's, eyebrows that curved downward at each end with bits of blonde hair above the bridge of his nose. He had the appealing looks of both. My boy also had my mother's smile—minus the gapped teeth.

"I don't like it that you don't go to church with us anymore. Now, we can't have pancakes for lunch. I like pancakes." He paused for a few seconds, then, licked his lips.

"Why do you think we won't have pancakes?" I asked.

"Cuz church is boring and that's the best part of Sunday—when we get home. If you don't go to church anymore, Sunday's no fun 'cuz the second best thing is that I get to lean on you and dream about pancakes 'til my mouth gets wet inside. It's so wet I have to wipe my mouth on your jacket 'cuz it comes down my chin. Remember, Mommy? You made me sit up when I did it the last time. And you told me that we wouldn't have pancakes if I didn't stop 'dooling.' I stopped 'dooling' last week and today."

I knelt down to give Cameron a hug; then another kiss on the top of his head, inhaling the baby shampoo I still used when I washed his hair.

It seemed that, for Cameron, pancakes were synonymous with the four of us going to church together after which he would receive his reward for sitting through a one-hour service.

Sunday school was not something offered by the church. A nursery was provided for infants and children three years or younger. The four-year-olds and older were expected to be in church with their parents.

It was Chuck who enjoyed making crêpes and pancakes for our family. It was something he did most Sundays when we returned from the morning church service. "Yes we will, because I'm going with you next Sunday—and all of the Sundays after that."

"So, we'll have pancakes next week?" he asked as he clapped his hands.

"Yup! We'll have them today, too. Daddy's coming into the kitchen in a few minutes to make them. You get the frying pan out of the drawer while I get the ingredients."

Cameron's eyes widened. His broad grin exposed the space where his two bottom baby teeth had once been.

I missed church for two consecutive weeks before I realized how selfish I was in not taking my family into consideration. Although, I didn't have a change of heart, I *had* made a commitment to Chuck to worship at the Canadian Reformed Church when we were married. I needed to honour that promise.

"I met with the minister of the Christian Reformed Church in

Newmarket, last week," I said to Chuck, earlier that morning, as we sat outside drinking our coffee on the deck.

"And...."

"When I sat down in his office to speak with him, I didn't know what to say. I felt as though I'd made a mistake by going there. It was an uncomfortable few minutes. I told him I wanted to leave Bethel and yet, while I was talking about how I wasn't being fed, I felt disloyal. I sensed he felt uncomfortable, too. He kept fidgeting in his chair, repeatedly shifting his legs and fingering his beard. I shouldn't have gone."

I put down my coffee mug, got up from the lounge chair and walked over to where Chuck sat.

"Stand up. I need to hug you."

When I leaned my head against his chest, I could hear the beat of his heart—the steady, rhythmic beat. It was a hot, humid summer day, but I was only aware of the comfort and security of being held by him.

"I'm relieved to hear that," Chuck said as he leaned his chin on my head.

"But, why" I asked, "did you say so little about it? Weren't you worried I would never go back to church with you and the kids?"

"Not really. I knew you would come to your senses."

"But how did *you* know when *I* didn't know myself?" I challenged.

"I know *you*, Claudia, that's why."

"Well, good for you, because I don't! And, I don't find your answer very satisfactory."

"It will have to do," he said. He turned, opened the sliding door to the kitchen and went inside. I remained on the second-storey deck observing our surrounding fields. Several of Chuck's Black Angus cows stood by the pond, greedily lapping up water.

Simple animals, simple needs. They're leaving—thirst quenched.

I stood with my elbows on the deck railing for a few more minutes, watching the last two head of cattle turn away from the pond. When they reached the rest of the herd, I turned, opened the sliding door and stepped into the kitchen. Cameron was standing on a stool with an egg in his hand. Chuck stood beside him.

"Careful not to get any eggshell in the batter. We want these to be perfect pancakes," cautioned Chuck.

Crack—*splat!*

"Oh, oh," whimpered Cameron as the slimy yellow yolk slid onto the white counter.

"Cameron, stop crying. We all have accidents and make mistakes. I'll get another egg from the fridge. You can try again," Chuck said as he walked toward the refrigerator door I was holding open for him.

"Mistakes, yes, they happen to everybody," I said.

I left the kitchen.

* * * * *

Though I held to my promise of attending church, during the four subsequent years, I once again became self-absorbed, busy with the activities I enjoyed most. I went back to York University, enrolled in my third photography class and picked up a couple of other courses with the intention of obtaining a degree in Fine Arts.

April 21, 1981

I've had a pretty good 1981 so far as my personal career is concerned. The story I wrote about "The Post Mistress of Kettleby" received an "A" in my Social Science course. My professor has suggested I publish it. I will if I can.

My photography has really taken off. I started my own business with business cards printed up in February. I have done work for Chuck and one of his law partners. Now in March and April, I am taking photos of Jaymor dance students. I also took photos for a big litigation case for John last week. I'm beginning slowly and can't take on any more work.

Chuck is having a darkroom built for me so I can process my own photos. I was going to take fourth year photography next year but those plans have fallen through.

Tamara has turned out to be a nightmare. I don't want to put the kids through another sitter so I'll just sit tight until Melinda is old enough to stay on her own and take care of Cameron herself. That will only be a couple of years away.

Despite my professor's suggestion, I didn't pursue the idea of trying to publish my story. In fact, I flitted from one interest to another. I did, however, put university on hold.

I found I couldn't stay focused on one thing for any length of time. I needed to be constantly on the move—not alone with my thoughts for too long. If I wasn't involved in something that consumed me, I became swathed in depression and turned inward. Self-recrimination chipped away at me like the sharp edge of an icepick. I became impatient with the children.

"Cameron, don't keep talking! I need to think," I said to my young son when I was driving him to school one morning.

"Okay," he said, as he leaned his body against the door of the car.

It wasn't until three days later, as I drove him to school again, that he said, "Is it okay if I talk now, Mommy?"

What am I doing to my kids? My children have to ask me if they can talk to me? I'm such a lousy mother.

If I could find something that I like enough and stick to it, I would be a better mother—I would be happier. I can't find anything.

Just because mine is a small business doesn't mean my photography work shouldn't be taken seriously. The lab is always messing up my orders. I feel like quitting—but what will I do with my time? Chuck works so much. I'm lonely. I want to move from the country—maybe settle in Aurora. Nah, Chuck won't go for it.

Even with my lapses into hopelessness, I seemed able to snap out of them and continue my involvement in various pursuits.

I threw myself into tennis: joined a tennis club, joined a tennis league, took innumerable lessons. I found local babysitters to stay with the children while I went out a few nights a week to play at the club.

I felt I had to prove something to myself. I became fanatical about tennis. It began to define who I was and I how I felt about myself. *We lost again!*

I hired babysitters to take care of the children when they were home from school and during the summer holidays.

25

A temporary diversion

When the Lord designs to work grace in a heart, and redeem a soul to himself, he first weans it from the world.[23]

1984
In the fall of 1984, I gave up tennis and flung myself into my photography business once more. That's when I decided to specialize in pet photography.

We live in King Township—horse country—many people here have pets, some two or three. I'm specializing. There should be lots of opportunity for business.

I took photographs of our black and brown German shepherd, Brandy, and our tortoise-coloured cat, Dora (our adopted cat that came with my mother's name). Chuck had given me a Mamiya RB67 professional camera for my birthday.

After I took photographs, I had the lab do prints in sizes ranging from 8" x 10" to 16" x 24". I also had samples of the photographs adhered to canvas. This gave the portraits an oil painting look. I called on pet store owners, veterinarians and tack shop owners. I asked if I could leave my framed samples for them to hang on their walls. Each took a stack of my cards. It generated business. I felt fulfilled—for a while.

My photography business flourished. People wanted portraits of their pets. It kept me busy and involved in something I thoroughly enjoyed.

I purchased additional equipment—lights, umbrellas, filters, various coloured canvas backdrops, a tripod and a light meter— all the tools to enable me to take photographs of pets in the homes of their owners. My portable studio worked well.

Dogs were easy subjects. The various sounds I mimicked generated the desired responses. I clicked my tongue, hissed, meowed and chirped. The sitting dog would cock his head to the left, to the right or look directly into the camera. I could take a photograph that made even the least intelligent breed of dog look scholarly.

Cats were more difficult. They were less co-operative than most dogs. Bribery wouldn't work. I carried catnip with me. Once the table, cushion and cat were creatively arranged on my custom-made portable wooden table, I would hand catnip to the pet owner. I usually procured only one pose from the cat—if I was lucky. While the owner dangled the catnip, the front paw and the head would rise up. No catnip received because…no cat! Off it would go into hiding. No amount of catnip or, "Here kitty, kitty," would coax the cat from its hiding place.

I stopped photographing cats after a Persian cat urinated on one of my umbrellas. The umbrella had been lying, rolled up, on the living room floor while I was loading my equipment in my Jeep Wagoneer. She had been sly about it. Maybe she was retaliating. It didn't really matter, I was through with cats.

26

Meeting Jesus

But God demonstrates his own love for us in this: While we were still sinners, Christ died for us (Romans 5:8, NIV).

1985
The Arlington Pet Shop, located in a strip plaza on Yonge Street in Newmarket, provided me with my best promotion. A dog breeder, John Mairs—from whom I purchased our German shepherd, Brandy—introduced me to the co-owners.

I had taken photographs of John's German shepherd, as well as a family portrait of him, his wife and two daughters. He liked my work and thought displaying my animal photographs at the pet shop would generate more business for me. John's introduction to those owners spawned considerably more than a new business opportunity.

It was early in August. Responding to a third invitation to return, I was arranging a display of animal photographs on the easels I brought to the Arlington Pet Shop.

I was distracted by an English bulldog. The smell—a pungent odor reminiscent of the swampy, sewage smell of the Florida Everglades —first caught my attention. When I turned to look at him, the wrinkled-faced dog had drool hanging from his jowls. He stopped midway through the open shop door and caught a glimpse of his own reflection in the window. He began to bark and growl, as though at a threatening rival.

"It's okay, boy. It's only you," said a young man while rubbing the dog's head. He knelt down to wipe his pet's mouth with a wad of tissue from his jeans' pocket.

"There you go—all dry."

The young man wrapped his arms around his pet and lifted him up. The dog nuzzled into his chest.

Such an unpleasant-looking dog. And smell? Yuck! Unconditional love, for sure.

As I turned back to my easel, I heard Dave, one of the owners, in conversation with a customer. "I have a video called *Jesus of Nazareth*, that I watch whenever I feel out of touch with God—when I need spiritual nourishment," said Dave.

Drawn by the conversation, I stepped toward them. "I sure could use some spiritual nourishment in my life," I blurted out. *Did I really say that? Where is this coming from?*

They both turned their attention toward me. *They're smiling at me. I just eavesdropped, but they don't seem to mind.*

"You're welcome to borrow my video, if you like. It is six hours long, by the way," Dave said.

"Sure—I would like to—if you don't mind."

Why am I so keen to sit for six hours and watch a video about the life of Jesus? It's summer. Daytime is for sunbathing and swimming. Evening is for sitting by the pool. I can't fit this in. Do I even want to? Still, I feel spiritually dead. I need to make the time!

"Oh, you'll need a Betamax. Do you own one?" inquired Dave.

"No, but I can probably get one from somewhere," I said.

"I'm away next weekend so you can borrow mine," he offered.

I feel eager to watch this movie. Why?

I looked at Dave and thought of how I judged him, how I looked down on him because of his scruffy appearance—his unkempt beard, his tousled thick wavy black hair. He always wore jeans and the same blue plaid shirt, and he looked as though he enjoyed his sweets just a little too much.

He is such an accommodating man: letting me set up my display without charge, speaking kindly to me even though I've been eaves-dropping. Now, he's offering me his video and his machine!

My cheeks felt hot. I looked down at the tile floor.

What if it's nice next weekend? I'd sure hate to borrow it and then not watch the video. But I may lose out on getting it again.

I looked up at him and returned his smile.

"Well, thank you; I appreciate it."

"I'll bring it to the store next Friday. You can drop by and take it home with you."

"It's an amazing movie!" said Dave as he bobbed up and down on the balls of his feet.

"It's very kind of you, thanks again."

The following weekend was sunny with temperatures in the mid-to-high 20s. I was determined to watch the video regardless of the pull of the outdoors. Chuck spent the morning baling hay while Cameron and Melinda watched cartoons downstairs in the family room. While they were occupied, I went into our bedroom and slipped the video into the machine.

By noon, Chuck came inside for lunch. The children were dressed in their bathing suits and sitting at the kitchen table eating their lunch of macaroni and cheese.

"Are you coming out with us to the pool, Mom?" Melinda asked before she licked the last bit of cheese from the back of her fork.

"Probably later on," I said.

"C'mon kids, let's go. You know your mother doesn't go into the pool more than once on the weekend," said Chuck.

"I think I made up for two weekends last night. I swam before supper *and* after—if you'll recall. I'll be out—just not now."

What's the problem that I can't tell my family that I'm watching a video about Jesus? I'm almost ashamed that I need to be doing this. Why?

"What's the big secret?" I can imagine Melinda saying to me. I can't even answer that question for myself.

It had been easy for me to watch it the day before. The kids had been next door at the Smids. Chuck had been out baling.

Okay, here it goes, the last segment. It's nothing that I don't already know. What is triggering this sudden interest?

For the next little while, I sat on our bed watching the build-up to Judas Iscariot's betrayal of Christ.

I grabbed a tissue and dabbed my eyes; my hands felt clammy. I folded one leg over the other and, leaning forward, placed my elbows on the bed, both fists scrunched under my jaw.

There he is—Jesus—wearing a crown of thorns.

He was despised and rejected by mankind,
  a man of suffering, and familiar with pain.
Like one from whom people hide their faces
  he was despised, and we held him in low esteem.
But he was pierced for our transgressions,
  he was crushed for our iniquities;
the punishment that brought us peace was on him,
  and by his wounds we are healed (Isaiah 53:3,5, NIV).

Oh—he's hanging from the cross!
Tears rolled down my cheeks. I let them flow. My hands felt clammy; my forehead, hot.
What's happening to me?
I fell back against the pillows as my chest heaved up and down. I couldn't look any longer at the scene unfolding on the television screen.
Where have I been? Why have I not given much thought about his sacrifice? Why have I never been touched by Jesus' death in this way? Words—they've only been words—spoken by a minister, read from the Bible. The words didn't penetrate my heart.
As I sat on our king size bed, I sniffed and blew my nose. For several minutes, I remained staring at the blank screen. It was over.
Something astounding happened while I was watching the movie. I was now convinced I was absolved of my own sins of thought, word and deed at the cross of Christ. I was lifted up and embraced by the One who loves me unconditionally.
Yes. All my sins were forgiven!

27

Changed

Therefore, if anyone is in Christ, he is a new creation: the old has gone, the new has come! (2 Corinthians 5:17, NIV).

1985
I feel so content; almost jubilant; no morning irritability.
I sauntered from the bedroom into the kitchen and poured a coffee; then, looked out of our glass double doors. On the grass, the August dew glistened like tiny crystals in the early morning sunshine.

Having finished my coffee, I tore down the hallway and into the family library which housed my office. On a shelf, I found what I was looking for: Calvin's *Institutes*, Volume 1. I looked at the first five pages. *Heavy reading, but it will have to do.*

I tucked the hardcover book under my arm, changed into my bathing suit in the bedroom and, book in hand, went outside to join my family by the pool.

Chuck stood watering the mauve petunias cascading from the clay pots hanging throughout our backyard. I watched Melinda swim the length of the pool, looking every bit like a swimming instructor—perfectly executing the maneuvers she learned at lessons the day before.

"Hi, Honey." Chuck said as he stood with hose in hand. "Did you get the coffee I left for you?"

"Yup, thank you."

"Watcha got under your arm?"

"Um, just thought I'd take a look at a book we had in our library."

He's so preoccupied with his flowers. He's not bothering to ask me the title. I'll wait until this evening and explain it all to him. Everyone's doing their own thing—I have some privacy, sort of.

God has left me without a doubt that my experience has been genuine. In the past, my emotions have had a tendency to mess with me. I've never been able to trust them. Now, though, I'm certain Jesus has saved me. He is the Lord of my life.

"Hi Mom," called out Cameron as he stood at the edge of the diving board in his dark brown bathing suit.

"Watch this!"

His cannonball managed to cool my hot skin. I threw my off-white towel over my shoulders and headed for the fire-engine red lounge chair. I wheeled the chair as far away from the family as possible. Once flat on my stomach, I began to read Chapter One. The sun felt good on my back. I nibbled away on every word, reading and re-reading until I had a clear understanding of its message. As I read, I became more convinced that what happened the day before had been real. My stomach flipped.

I need to go to the Treasure House Bookstore and buy a Christian book to take on our trip to Europe next week. I want to swim with the tide taking me to the unknown places of faith in Christ.

That evening, when the children were both asleep, I sat down with Chuck in our living room. I told him about the movie *Jesus of Nazareth*—how it had affected me while I watched it over the weekend. When I finished, Chuck remained silent for a few minutes.

"I can see that I made assumptions I shouldn't have made about your commitment," he said, while he stroked his chin.

"Well, you shouldn't have. You needed to talk to me, Chuck."

"I knew you were rebelling over the orthodoxy of the church. I knew you thought it was rigid, but…."

"I was. I still find it rigid. But I like Pastor Gleason—he's different, and he's not Dutch. I like Americans—they're open. I like his wife, Sally. I want to get to know her better. The Dutch traditions seem to be just that—traditions."

"Don't forget your own roots, Claudia. You were comfortable in the Anglican Church, and it's steeped in tradition."

"...and two services on a Sunday are excessive," I responded. "I never had to attend twice on Sunday at the Anglican Church."

While we were talking, my head was spinning. Even as I commented negatively about the two services on Sunday, I started thinking it may be a good idea: another opportunity to worship God and to expand my knowledge of his truths. I needed to really listen.

"I think you're confusing value systems with culture," said Chuck. Later, I would come to understand what Chuck said was true—not only that, I came to appreciate it!

For years, I had believed I was a committed Christian. Not one to openly talk about his faith, Chuck had thought so, too.

★ ★ ★ ★ ★

During the summer of my "road to Damascus" experience, I was quiet about my conversion. I *didn't* rush out and tell all of my friends and family about the joys found in Christ, as I thought I would. I felt I needed to expand my knowledge regarding the things of God. The desire to know more about him propelled me toward reading books that would help me understand what exactly had happened to me on that August weekend as I watched the film, *Jesus of Nazareth.*

On the day following that experience, I drove to the Treasure House Bookstore in Newmarket. Melinda was in charge of Cameron, so I knew I could be a while at the bookstore.

Traffic along Highway 9 was stop-and-go. I could see there was an accident up ahead. Police were erecting barricades to reroute the traffic which now came to a complete stop.

Curious, like others in their vehicles around me, I strained to see ahead. I began to pray, but for whom? Those who may be injured. Patiently, I waited for a while, thinking. *God has done so much for me, what can I do for him? But, I have nothing to offer—no particular talent.*

I found a book I felt was just right for me: *Beyond Ourselves* by Catherine Marshall. I was attracted to it because it was easy to understand. I felt I had to begin with the fundamentals of the

Christian faith and build upon that knowledge. I became convinced I had to pray the "sinner's prayer" to be exonerated from my sin and forgiven. In reading Marshall's book, I took my cue from an illustration she used when writing about another's quest for forgiveness of sins through Jesus Christ.

I remember that date: August 28, 1985. When we returned from our two week vacation in Europe, I had finished the book. Alone in my room, I sat on the bed and said my prayer of faith: "Jesus, I know I have sinned against you and need your forgiveness. Please come into my life and forgive my sin. Change me into the person that you intended for me to be. Amen."

★ ★ ★ ★ ★

As my new life in Christ began, I continued to journal my experiences in anticipation of the changes I could expect.

Along with conversion, there came the realization that I now had a Father whom I could trust. Nothing I needed would be hidden from me. God's Word had become, indisputably, "a lamp unto my feet."[24]

"Never will I leave you; never will I forsake you"[25]

August 28, 1985
I have a strong desire to pray. Every day I have a feeling of joy. God has given me strength during the times when I don't sleep at night. I enjoy doing things for my family and friends more than I ever have in my life. There is a constant need to read of God's goodness.

28

A new direction

And you also were included in Christ when you heard the message of truth, the gospel of your salvation. When you believed, you were marked in him with a seal, the promised Holy Spirit, who is a deposit guaranteeing our inheritance until the redemption of those who are God's possession—to the praise of his glory (Ephesians 1:13–14, NIV).

1985

In the summer of 1985, Nancy Vanderkooi stood staring at me. She reached out and touched my arm.

"That's nice of you, Claudia, but you don't need to drive Kevin home later. You'll have him for the whole day. You're doing me a favour by having him here."

Kevin was one of Cameron's good friends. The two ten-year-olds were going together into grade five at the Holland Marsh District Christian School. Kevin came from a large Dutch Canadian family who lived in Holland Marsh a few kilometers north of us. They were good people—dedicated to their Reformed faith as well as their church and family. They had suffered the loss of a two-year-old son who had choked on a carrot while sitting in his high chair eating his afternoon snack—something any mother would have a hard time dealing with. I hadn't met Nancy before she lost her son, but she always struck me as a strong, solid Christian woman whose faith never wavered no matter what her circumstances. How I admired her.

So many years ago, how would I have handled such a tragedy? I would have blamed God for taking my child from me—that's how I would have reacted.

"Nancy, I'm driving him home. I'm more than happy to do it," I gently responded.

I want to hug this woman right now and tell her what happened to me! She's a committed lady—she'll be pleased. But no…not yet. Besides, she knows I'm a Christian, even if she doesn't know how superficial my faith had become.

Nancy tilted her head and smiled, "Thanks, Claudia. I'll be home all day. Drop him off any time."

She sees I'm different. I know she does, just by the way she's looking at me. I have to tell all my friends right away. Dad—he needs to know, too—my family, everyone I love!

Once conversion took place, the pitch of my excitement was constant. I needed to tone it down and take things as I should: with the steady rhythm of learning about God through his Word while continuing to grow in my Christian walk. The more I learned about God, his forgiveness and his love for me, the more I soared to elevated heights of delight.

I boldly stated the gospel message to each of my non-believing friends. Although most disagreed with me or politely listened, each one continued to be my friend.

When I engaged in conversation with others—those known to me or not—I would eventually interject my perspective on faith.

"Well, the *person* I am speaking about is Jewish, and he's a better Christian than anyone I know who claims to be one!" said the man who had the misfortune of sitting next to me at a wedding reception.

I sucked in my breath but *did not* say, "How is that possible if he's Jewish?"

Chuck, I recall, raised his eyebrows as he leaned over the white linen tablecloth and looked at me. I knew I'd taken it too far. But, I was hopping mad that I couldn't complete the conversation and defend my position.

Naively, I believed anyone with whom I shared the gospel message would want what I had.

★ ★ ★ ★ ★

September 5, 1986
I look back on the year and can see that daily prayer, plus a quiet
time with God, is the only way to maintain a positive outlook in
living from day to day. My faith has never once weakened. Again,
prayer is the strongest factor in maintaining and improving my
spiritual life. It's reflected in my day-to-day behaviour—my atti-
tude toward everything and everyone.

September 15, 1986
I need to belong to a Christian ladies' group. I called Joan H. today
about joining a Bible study, but she wasn't home and didn't return
my call. I have to pursue someone else to help me out. I know if I
don't start with a group soon, I'll eventually give up trying, even
though I really want to do it and know that I need to belong to one
in order to grow.

September 16, 1986
What an experience I had today. I called Joan again and asked
her to suggest a Bible study group for me. Eva (a lady I met at the
Beacon Bible Camp weekend) mentioned me to a woman from
Aurora. In the end, both Joan and Eva (who do not know one
another) told this lady about me. Her name is Carol Ford. She
called me. I marvel at the work of the Lord. I'm very interested in
seeing what he has in mind for me.

"I figured I needed to contact you right away after two people on
the same day called me and gave me your name," said Carol during
our phone conversation.

Carol ran the Bible study in her home. That week, a group of
five women sat around her dining room table studying God's
Word together. Afterward, Carol asked if there were any prayer
requests. There were. I listened while each woman spoke to God
as though he was present in the room. Old feelings of insecurity
created a barrier that hindered my focus.

Please Lord, teach me to pray like these ladies. Open my mouth.

"I have a prayer request," I said as the ladies began putting on their jackets to leave. "Would all of you please pray that I may learn to pray also—the way you all do—I mean out loud?"

"Let's do that right now," suggested Carol. "We'll go into the living room and sit on the couch together."

All agreed.

I felt splotches of perspiration seeping through my cotton blouse.

"You sit here in the middle, Claudia," said Claire as we stood near the sofa. As the five of us sat, Carol took my one hand and Claire, the other.

This feels so strange—holding hands and all. Please God help me to relax and be comfortable with this.

They each petitioned my request, giving their own words to every appeal.

I had faith the prayers would be answered. *After all, God will want this, too.*

* * * * *

September 19, 1986
I spoke with Eva yesterday. She can be such an inspiration to me. I am looking forward to seeing her in two weeks at the monthly meeting of Christian Women's Club.[26] *I feel good all over thinking about belonging to CWC and also heading up the church library which Sally Gleason has encouraged me to do. I think they are both exciting steps toward growth in my life.*

September 26, 1986
This has been one of the most exciting weeks for me. I have never felt God's presence in my life as strongly as I have these past seven days. I'm working very hard to please him. I have my struggles but God is taking care of them one by one as well as my weaknesses, such as my periodic negative emotional outbursts. I have committed everything to him. It has made temptation for me much easier to ignore and not to give in to. Every day is full of surprises. They are mini miracles to me!

September 28, 1986
Yesterday, I decided I'm going to witness to Dad. I felt very strongly

about it. I read Hebrews this morning and will start from there.
When I told Melinda, she said she has been praying and was
pleased I'm doing it. I'll have to pray about this all day today.
Tomorrow I'm going to Welland for a visit.

> *"The son is the radiance of God's glory and the exact represen-*
> *tation of his being, sustaining all things by his powerful word.*
> *After he had provided purification for sins, he sat down at the*
> *right hand of the Majesty in heaven." Hebrews 1:3.*

September 30, 1986
I talked to Mom and Dad for an hour and a half yesterday. Dad
listened as did Mom as I explained my conversion experience. I
told them both about the change in me. I told Dad how he could
enrich his life by reading the Bible every day. Mom said they
would do it over breakfast. We spoke of my faith openly. Poor Dad
didn't get his lunch until 1:30 p.m. I don't know how much he got
out of all that I said but he did tell me he believed in God and Jesus
and that sometimes he has prayed. It was a wonderful day!

★ ★ ★ ★ ★

Not long after we met, Carol Ford and I had become good friends.
She always invited me to the monthly meeting of the Christian
Women's Club. In addition, she also included me in anything
where Christian women would be gathered. Carol knew I craved
the company of those who were like-minded. One such occasion
prompted an invitation to attend a seminar where I would be introduced to yet another group of women.

"The meeting is geared toward women who would like to put
their testimony of faith together," said Carol. "It's sure to be a good
morning. You'll meet more Christian women even if the 'speaking'
topic doesn't interest you."

"It definitely doesn't."

At one point, halfway through the meeting, Carol, who sat next
to me, leaned in and whispered, "Sorry Claudia, I had no idea we
would be required to speak. I guess I should have known attending a speakers' seminar would mean some kind of participation."

"But, I couldn't say anything more than my name and where I lived. I was supposed to talk about myself for one minute!" *I must stop whining.* "Never mind, it doesn't matter. I have no intention of doing this again. It's been an interesting morning. The women have been easy to talk with. Over and above the painful speaking exercise, I enjoyed myself."

In the meantime, a middle-aged lady, seated to my left, tapped me on my arm after I sat down following my embarrassing moment. "Not everyone is gifted to speak, dear."

Understated!

★ ★ ★ ★ ★

A few months later, after a Christian Women's Club meeting in Aurora, I was getting ready to leave. A familiar-looking woman with close-cropped dark hair, dressed in a navy blue suit walked toward me. She smiled as she extended her right hand. Although somewhat bewildered by her gesture, I extended mine. She clasped my hand in both of hers.

Her face looks familiar—but from where? Should I know her? I don't think so. It seems that everyone I meet from the Christian community exudes warmth—at least here at Christian Women's Club.

"I remember you from the speakers' seminar," said the woman. She introduced herself as she continued to grip my hand.

My smile vanished.

"Have you thought about speaking?" she inquired.

She must have me confused with someone else.

"Not at all. I couldn't even put a sentence together. Remember?"

"No, I don't recall that."

She tilted her head back and looked up at the ceiling as though trying to recollect the incident.

"I do remember you, but I don't recollect that you didn't speak."

Thank you, Lord, for small mercies.

As she lowered her head, she looked at me and said, "I'm going to put my testimony on tape and send it in to Daisy Cross. She picks the speakers for Christian Women's." Her broad smile radiated her pleasure.

"You're going to speak? You're brave."

I may have just insulted her—one more reason why I should never speak. My foot usually finds its way to my mouth!

"Only if Daisy approves my testimony," she went on. "My friends have encouraged me to go ahead with it."

Now I remember her. She was one of those confident ladies who spoke with ease.

"You'll never see me giving my testimony...or speaking anywhere for that matter."

I grabbed my raincoat from the hanger and slipped it on. The woman was still standing beside me as I began buttoning up my coat.

Grinning at me, she raised her finger and wagged it in front of my face. "You never know."

Oh, yes I do. This is good, I'm practicing restraint.

"All the best to you. I'll look forward to seeing you up at the podium one day."

29

Observations

Heart-godliness pleases God best, and life-godliness honours him most. In a godly man's heart, though some sin is left, no sin is liked; in his life, though sin remains, yet no sin reigns.[27]

1986

"Mom, you've changed."

Melinda stood before me in the kitchen wearing her plaid, below-the-knee length skirt. Her matching pink headband held back the curls of her freshly permed brown hair. We were practically nose to nose. Melinda stood about three inches away from my face scrutinizing me as though she had just found a zit forming above my upper lip.

"Why have you got that look on your face? What's so amusing?"

"Oh, I was just thinking how you used to say inappropriate things—and those songs you used to sing!" said Melinda, grabbing her lunch bag.

"Such as...."

"Can't talk now. I have to get going or I'll miss the school bus. Bye."

"Wait...wait...what kind of inappropriate things?"

She rapidly tapped down the steps like Ginger Rogers about to fling herself into the arms of Fred Astaire.

The front door banged. She was gone. I didn't have a clue as to what constituted "inappropriate" in the mind of my fifteen-year-old daughter. I could barely remember what I had been like before Christ entered my life and took hold of my soul.

★ ★ ★ ★ ★

I was sitting at the kitchen table when Melinda returned from school that day. *Do I really want to know what I used to say or sing that Melinda deems inappropriate? Well, I must want to know because I've been thinking about it all day!*

"Cameron," I shouted as he whizzed by the kitchen door without saying, "Hello." Wash those hands before you come into the kitchen!"

"Mom, what do you think I'm doing? I could smell the chocolate chip cookies as soon as I opened the front door! Yum, I'm drooling. Oh, I left a big spot on the rug. Really, I drooled all the way up the stairs," said my son, who has the same weird sense of humour as my dad.

Melinda sat down after she poured herself a glass of milk. She began dunking her cookie, leaving little bits of crumbs and chocolate floating on top.

"Your grandmother never let me dunk my cookies."

"Mom, you're starting to repeat yourself."

"Just want to remind you of how good you have it."

Melinda stopped mid-bite and rolled her eyes. *She's such a teenager.*

"Now, back to our discussion of this morning," I said.

"Our discussion…?"

"You know: 'the inappropriate things' I used to say and sing."

Brace yourself, Claudia—why don't I remember?

"It was the *songs* you used to sing, mostly."

At the top of her lungs, after swallowing all of her cookie and taking a gulp of milk, she began, "Cigarettes and whiskey and wild, wild, women. They'll drive you crazy, they'll drive you in-s-a—a-ne."

"That was just a funny song I picked up from Uncle Bob," I said. "It was silly."

"Oh, and here's another one—much worse—you won't like this, Mom."

"Never mind, never mind. I'll work harder at cleaning up the inappropriate, sorry."

"Mom, you already have, that was my point."

30

Craig

Faith finds mercy in the greatest affliction and in the saddest
mixture of providence. Praise God for past mercies and it will
not be long before you have a new song in your mouth for the
present mercy.[28]

In 1987, when Craig's erratic behaviour had started to surface, he
was urged by Carl to seek counselling. At that time, he agreed to
it. His own family doctor, a woman, began seeing Craig for his
psychological problems. We were relieved to know he pursued this,
but as he drifted further and further away from the family, there
wasn't any indication of how effective it was.

One evening that year, Craig stood in my kitchen watching me
prepare dinner for him and our family.

There isn't much I remember regarding our conversation, but
at one point when I looked up at him, he was staring straight
ahead into the black face of my microwave oven as though it held
some great fascination for him.

"What are you thinking about, Craig?"

Slowly his eyes shifted. He stared directly at me. His pupils
appeared like tiny dots in a sea of blue. "I imagine myself as being
homeless someday—living on the streets."

"What?" I said. "Are you kidding? Why would you think such a
thing?"

Craig turned toward the hallway door.

"It's just a feeling I have, is all," he said as he looked over his shoulder at me.

"A feeling based on what?" I asked, holding the wooden spoon in mid-air. The gravy trickled down onto my hand.

Craig stopped, turned around and looked at me. His round smooth baby face appeared drawn and taut. I felt a chill as though a cold wind had blown through the kitchen door.

"Well—Dad would be in the gutter if it weren't for Mom."

"But, Craig, you aren't like Dad—not at all."

"I guess not," he said as he turned and walked toward the kitchen door.

"Uh, no, you are not!" I yelled after him.

"Probably not."

Once Craig left the kitchen, I began to shake. My stomach went into knots.

What's going on? What's this all about? I have to speak to him as soon as we have some private time together.

The gravy in the pan turned thick and dark. I raised the wooden spoon to my mouth and tasted it. It had turned bitter. The smell of burnt food lingered.

★ ★ ★ ★ ★

"Craig's been fired from his job at the CBC," said Trisha. "He's moved back to Welland and is living with Mom and Dad."

Her voice sounded flat—emotionless.

I covered the mouthpiece with my hand and sighed. Little beads of perspiration dampened my brow.

"When did this happen? Mom never mentioned it to me when I spoke with her the other day. How can that be? *Why* would *Craig* get fired?"

"He assaulted his boss in the parking lot before work last week. Apparently, the first time he did it...."

"Wait a minute—he's done it *before*?"

"Calm down—let me finish," continued Trisha. "He struck his boss because he had teased Craig. I understand his boss started in on him again."

"He teased him about what? Do you know?"

"Craig won't talk about it."

"Did his boss press charges?" I knew the pitch of my voice was rising again.

Pause.

"Sorry, Trish," I said as I took a deep breath.

"No. He fired him on the spot."

"Who told you this?"

"Mom. I just got off the phone with her. She said she's glad he's come home."

I thought of Craig comparing himself to our dad when he'd been over for dinner. When I next talked with Craig, he said living with our parents was temporary, "Just until I find another job."

★ ★ ★ ★ ★

Craig never looked for another job. Instead, he spent his time trying to promote the making of a horror movie and threw himself into militant homosexual causes. He became increasingly delusional, badgering people for money and borrowing money from people he knew he couldn't repay. At one point, Shirley discovered there was little food in the house. Since Shirley also helped Mom with her banking she saw that Mom's bank account had been depleted by cheques made out to Craig. When the money ran out, Craig moved to Winnipeg.

31

A new desire

Praise be to the God and Father of our Lord Jesus Christ, the Father of compassion and the God of all comfort, who comforts us in all our troubles, so that we can comfort those in any trouble with the comfort we ourselves receive from God (2 Corinthians 1:3–4, NIV).

February 5, 1988
I have decided to become a volunteer counsellor at the Crisis Pregnancy Centre. It was a difficult decision for me to make, particularly in light of the fact that groups like these are considered fanatical. I have never really stood up and spoken out about my convictions on anything particularly controversial, as it does open up a person for attack. I pray that you, Lord, will give me the right words when necessary.

I longed to be used by God in some way. It was as though I expected him to drastically change the course of my life in one fell swoop. Since I was unsuccessful in my attempts to convert some of my friends and family members (plus a few strangers at social functions), I felt I now knew God hadn't given me the gift of evangelizing. *Okay, so I won't become a champion of Christ on the streets of Toronto.*

I had much to learn about the sovereignty of God and his will in the life of the believer.

February 6, 1988
Lord, you have spoken so clearly to me through your Word. It has
strengthened my faith and encouraged me to do what is right. Your
words are comforting and full of insight. I continue to praise and
thank you with love and (hopefully) obedience.

The one place I had freedom to talk about Christ was at the Crisis Pregnancy Centre in Toronto. There had been a notice in our church bulletin for women who wanted to attend a training program in order to become a counsellor at the centre. I took the course. At its completion, I felt I could be an effective counsellor. I had the desire, the opportunity and the ability. My insecure feelings were gradually waning. While at the training session, the women were asked to role play the client/counsellor positions. I felt comfortable and confident.

For the next five years, I volunteered at the centre. The work was fulfilling. Each week, before the first client came in, the director and two other volunteers would surround the individual counsellor who would be having an appointment with a client, and they would pray for her for the session.

The prayers of my Bible study group had been answered. I was able to pray audibly with ease. I felt capable and competent in presenting the gospel message.

The public knew the centre was a Christian organization. Often I prayed with the young ladies who were brought to me, but only after I asked their permission. Usually, I would only see these young women once. Some returned for follow-up, some decided to keep their babies. I did what I was trained to do: counsel the women against abortion and speak to them about putting their trust in Jesus Christ.

32

A forgiving heart

Bear with each other and forgive whatever grievances you may have against one another. Forgive as the Lord forgave you" (Colossians 3:13, NIV).

Where my father was concerned, my heart of stone had become a heart of flesh. As I listened to the sermons preached each Sunday, attended Bible study and prayed, I became aware that I no longer had an unforgiving attitude toward Dad. My loathing was replaced by love, as I began to realize we were *both* broken people. His brokenness played out in a self-destructive way—a way that included victims, our family. But I also came to learn that sin is sin. With some, it's more visible; with others, less so or completely hidden from human view—like my own sins, too numerous to count.

Although I had forgiven Dad, any outward display of affection toward him was always tentative at best. But, however awkward it felt, the first time I visited Dad after my conversion, I kissed him lightly on the cheek when I said my good-byes before leaving. I didn't look at him to see his reaction but turned and quickly darted down the front steps and onto the sidewalk, moving briskly toward my parked car. It felt odd to have this connection after physically distancing myself from him for so many years—the one exception being after John had broken off our engagement.

I started my car while both of my parents stood at the top of the steps. I could see them in my rearview mirror, watching my vehicle until it disappeared around the corner of Oakland Avenue and Elm Street. They had only started this ritual in recent months. As I observed them, I felt comforted. It seemed a natural way for parents to send a daughter off. Finally, I was experiencing both Mom and Dad in an intimate and loving way.

33

Godly alternatives

I can do everything through him who gives me strength
(Philippians 4:13, NIV).

1988
I'd never dealt well with disappointment. When a photography
exhibition at the Upper Canada Mall in Newmarket was can-
celled, I was left feeling discouraged with respect to my business.
Now what?
I sat at the desk in my office tapping my cheek with my index
finger while staring down at the black phone. Brooding over my
loss, I continued to rapidly press and depress the end of the ball
point pen I was clutching in my left hand. Eventually, it broke,
sprang into the air and landed in pieces beside my chair.
Immediately, I sensed God was about to pick me up and dust
me off, putting my pieces together—I could start all over again.
Surely God was waiting in the wings for me to clear out the clutter
—I needed to be prepared for whatever was to come next.
As I began tidying up my desk—still feeling somewhat discouraged—I picked up a pile of customer receipts. Under the heap, I
spotted a brochure given to me by a woman I met at a Christian
event. I had communicated my story of faith to her.
"Claudia, you have an important message to share with others,"
the middle-aged lady had commented.

She handed me the pamphlet and encouraged me to attend a "Speak Up with Confidence" seminar. I now had no choice but to pursue this new avenue in my life. After all, I was praying for God to show me the path he wanted me to take. I felt I knew him well enough to discern that God uses various people to bring about his will in the life of the believer.

★ ★ ★ ★ ★

With the receiver between my right shoulder and ear, I dialed the number on the pamphlet.

"Hello—Carol Kent speaking."[29]

Reaching the seminar leader directly nearly rendered me speechless.

"Oh...hello...Carol. My name is Claudia Loopstra. I would like to book you for the next weekend you have available for a 'Speak Up with Confidence' seminar.

"One second, Claudia. I have my schedule here in front of me."

I could feel my face flush.

Am I crazy? Me organize a seminar on speaking? Or on anything? This is definitely coming from God!

"Claudia, I have this upcoming May 26th to 28th weekend available." I could feel the warmth of her smile as she spoke.

"Wonderful," I said, as I twirled back and forth on my office chair.

"I require that you have 35 people registered. A church setting is best—less expensive to rent. Also, I will need three rooms where the attendees can split up into groups, with lecterns provided."

My leg jiggled up and down as I listened to Carol's "to do" list.

Lord, I trust you regarding this. If you are backing me—and I feel certain you are—I know you will bring in the people. I have only two months to get this together!

One week before the seminar, I had thirty people registered. I had called every Christian who I thought might be interested. It surprised me to learn how many women wanted to take Carol's course.

My final list of people came from various sources. Often the person I contacted would recommend someone else who would likely be interested as well.

Over the next two months, I was in constant communication with God. He had been teaching me to "pray continually."[30]

May 11, 1988
I pray, with all my heart, the Carol Kent seminar will take place. Guide me, Lord. It needs to happen here. I trust you will help me to do what is necessary.

As of May 19, I had only thirty people. I called Carol.
"Thirty people will be fine, Claudia," Carol assured me. It was confirmed. Carol would arrive on Thursday afternoon, May 26th.

★ ★ ★ ★ ★

After an exhilarating weekend of learning how to develop skills in public speaking, I was ready to utilize all I had been taught by Carol Kent.
"I suggest, Claudia, you put your personal testimony of faith together and send it to me on a cassette tape," encouraged Carol. "You can do this. You have the tools now, plus the talent."
I have never before heard that word used to describe me!
Knowing this was something I felt led to do, I believed God would be with me throughout my preparation and on into my actual speaking engagements.
While I still had insecurities about my own capabilities, I had complete trust in God.

★ ★ ★ ★ ★

It was August 1988, when Chuck, Melinda, Cameron and I were taking a trip through Europe. With black spiral notebook in hand, I sat in the back seat of our rented vehicle and started to write about how, in 1985, God had revealed himself to me. Like soil soaked by a sprinkler, the pages, as I wrote, became drenched with a blessing of words used to describe God's saving grace in my life. I wanted to convey to others how changes in my life began to surface following my conversion experience. When satisfied I had included all that was essential to communicate—particularly stressing the act of forgiveness through Christ's death on the cross—I closed my notebook and waited until I returned home to record my testimony. Then, I would send my tape to Carol Kent, as she suggested.

I wanted this to be as professional and clear as possible. I'd been told about a Christian studio in Toronto where I could get my message recorded. When I returned home from Europe, I made the appointment and drove to Toronto. I was set up with a microphone. A technician wore earphones as he recorded my message in his small glassed-in studio. When I was finished my half-hour delivery, it was confirmed, once again, that this was what God wanted me to do.

"Your testimony is important. You should be telling your story."

I thanked him for his encouraging words and said I would be sending in the tape to be approved, as I hoped to speak for the Christian Women's Club.

Carol was sent a copy of the tape. The other went to Daisy Cross, the person I knew was responsible for selecting speakers for the Christian Women's Club.

December 16, 1988
I received a letter from Daisy. She liked it and approved me as a speaker. Thank you, Lord! Now I can agree with the words of the woman I'd met at CWC—"You never know!"

Despite all of the encouragement I received regarding my testimony, I still vacillated with respect to my self-confidence and, I suppose, complete trust in what God wanted me to do. He was dealing with a weak vessel.

I remembered a verse from Scripture—something Carol Kent had spoken about with regard to a person's capabilities. I jotted the following down in my journal at the time and found myself going back to it often.

"My grace is sufficient for you, for my power is made perfect in weakness" (2 Corinthians 12:9, NIV).

Also noted was Carol's perspective on this:

I believe the Christian who knows the power of God and is willing to give his or her potential to him, will live in the humble realization that God often allows the person with little natural ability to do his greatest work.

I memorized 2 Corinthians 12:9.

* * * * *

Being on the circuit for CWC brought many opportunities to witness about my faith in Jesus Christ. My energy level was at full-throttle as, over the next five years, I travelled from Espanola, Sudbury and North Bay, to southern Ontario and the Niagara Peninsula. I gained confidence, as I continued to deliver my message two or three times a month. I loved talking to women and encouraging them in their faith. The confidence I needed was generously given to me by God. Used of him, I became a strong vessel. All I was able to share openly, I attributed to the work of the indwelling Holy Spirit. To him, all glory was given.

Even as I witnessed effectively about my faith to others, I was still concerned about my own father. Mom told me she and Dad read the Bible and prayed every day. I was thrilled at the news. However, although I continued to grow in my faith, I had not yet grasped that not all who are committed to Christ experience faith in the same way. Nor do they wear their faith on their shirt sleeve as I did. I remained confused about Dad. His behaviour did not seem to be consistent with a man who believed. He still cussed and talked nastily to my mother. He continued to exhibit grumpiness and, at times, wouldn't communicate at all.

How soon I forgot that Dad suffered from clinical depression.

My father once told me he had attended a Billy Sunday revival in Buffalo, New York. According to Dad, when there was an altar call, he walked up to the front. His brother, Lionel, who was sitting next to him, looked up as Dad stood. Lionel shook his head in disbelief.

Like Uncle Lionel, I couldn't seem to accept the fact that Dad might have truly repented. His complex character, with constant changes in his behaviour, continued to leave me in doubt. Despite this, I never gave up encouraging him.

By late 1988, it was apparent to the family that our mother—who was in her late seventies—was showing mild symptoms of dementia. Shirley noticed her forgetfulness first, as she saw Mom the most. (Shirley lived in St. Catharines which is close to Welland.)

"When you think Dad and I are ready to go into a nursing home, we would like to live in Sunset Haven—just like my mother. They were awfully good to her there," Mom said to Shirley and me one afternoon when we were both visiting.

I looked at Dad. His eyes darted about the living room.

"Dad," I asked, "how do you feel about it?"

"Whatever your mother thinks is best. But I don't want to leave the old homestead, Claudia." He began rocking back and forth in the oak veneer rocking chair my grandfather had someone make for my grandmother.

"You understand you may have to leave someday, don't you?"

He nodded.

I grabbed a tissue off the end table and blew my nose.

Shirley told me she was also concerned about Dad because he had become totally dependent upon Mom for his care. His personality had mellowed somewhat but he, too, was showing signs of cognitive decline.

When Shirley went into Welland each Wednesday for a visit or to take Mom shopping, she found Mom often repeating herself within the first five minutes of a conversation. But, there were much bigger concerns.

One afternoon, after Shirley arrived at the house, Mom told Dad to sit on a dining room chair before she and Shirley left to go out. Shirley asked her why she was ordering Dad sit on the hard oak dining room chair. "I have to tie him up," she said.

Alarm bells clanged in Shirley's head.

"Calmly, I asked Mom why," Shirley related to me later on.

Mom explained that the last time she left Dad alone—when she went out with Aunt Violet, her best friend—she came back to the house to discover Dad was nowhere to be found. A while later she heard a knock on the door. There stood a taxi driver with Dad on the steps behind him. Dad told Mom he needed a haircut—but he had gone to the barber just the week before. Dad's barber, Joe,

Melinda, Mom, Dad and Cameron, Christmas 1988.

had known him for years. Joe called a taxi, paid the fare and sent him home.

As Shirley watched, Dad sat down on the chair as Mom instructed. Shirley asked Mom no further questions. She wanted to watch how this scene would unfold. Mom headed up the stairs while Dad sat with his head bowed, staring at the floor—waiting.

When she came down again, with three colourful ties in her hand, Shirley explained that she couldn't tie Dad up and leave him unattended. "What if there's a fire?"

That day, Dad shuffled along behind Mom and Shirley as they went grocery shopping.

A few days after speaking with Carl, Trisha and me, Shirley called the administrative office at Sunset Haven and requested an assessment on Mom and Dad. We all felt it was time to take measures to speed up the process of moving Mom and Dad into Sunset Haven. Shirley left a message for Craig to inform him of their impending move, but he didn't return her call. Mom explained that Craig had moved to Winnipeg. He had connected with someone regarding his movie—someone who was interested in the subject matter.

34

Leaving 56 Oakland Avenue

"Do not let your hearts be troubled. You believe in God; believe also in me. My Father's house has many rooms; if that were not so, would I have told you that I am going there to prepare a place for you? And if I go and prepare a place for you, I will come back and take you to be with me that you also may be where I am" (John 14:1–3, NIV).

1989
"Mom and Dad have to move into Sunset Haven by Thursday—a room for them has become available." The anxiety I caught in Shirley's voice nudged a quick response.

"I'll pack my bag and drive to Welland tomorrow."

Shirley made the phone call to me in late January 1989, while I was volunteering at the Crisis Pregnancy Centre. She had been told when a room became available at the home, Mom and Dad would have only one day to prepare. That day had arrived. My sister and I decided to go together, give them the news and stay overnight. Our intention was to make this transition go as smoothly as possible. We would pack their suitcases and drive them to their new home. Mom and Dad had been prepared for this day, but it still somewhat unnerved me to think of what their reaction would be as the move became a reality.

I arrived on a blustery winter day, before Shirley. My car inched its way up to crunch against the side of a pile of glistening snow in front of 56 Oakland Avenue. I sat for a few minutes thinking about some of the better times I had experienced since Dad mellowed and quit drinking. He was full of stories—stories that would sometimes make my sides ache from laughter.

One, in particular, came to mind. I recalled the day Dad and I sat together on the brown corduroy sofa in their living room. Although, I offered to help my hospitable and independent mother, she came into the room carrying three cups of steaming hot tea on a tray on which Dad had painted an arrangement of yellow and red roses.

My father discovered his artistic talent late in life—in his early sixties. He primarily used pastels as the medium for his finished product, although I remember he also used watercolour and oils for the many paintings he did of flowers—particularly, of roses.

As we sat and sipped our tea, Dad resumed his storytelling.

"Yup, I remember a time when your mother and I used to play cards with Violet, Scotty and two other couples. We would go to different houses every other month. One night, in the middle of our game of 500, one of the fellows excused himself from the table and opened the French doors leading to the living room. He closed the doors quietly behind him, stood there for a few seconds and then let out an explosion of gas. Everybody heard. He didn't realize there was no glass in the doors!

A few of us stared down at the cards. Some of us didn't want to embarrass him. The women looked away from the tables either disgusted or to stifle laughter. I dunno. I couldn't see their faces. When he came back in I said, 'Do you feel better now, Charlie?' His mouth fell open and then even the women laughed."

As I sat in the car, I chuckled at the memory of his story. Dad always liked to make people laugh. I imagine he'd "inflated" that one somewhat, although Mom never corrected him. She would have if he made it up.

My father's sense of humour was, at times, bizarre. He clearly had a creative bent.

"Dad, why do you have part of a woman's body pasted to the back wall of your bedroom?" I asked on one of my visits.

I walked over to the corner of the wall where he had glued a glossy picture of a woman's body from the waist down, in horizontal position. It started at the corner as though the upper part of the body continued beyond the wall.

Dad raised his eyebrows as though I didn't get it. I didn't.

"Why, I like the way the flare in her green skirt drapes over her calf. Don't you think her red high heel shoe looks elegant on that leg?"

"That's weird, Dad. Good thing you keep your door closed most of the time. Where did you find it?"

He told me his friend Harry Jerome, the next door neighbour, had passed along a stash of old magazines he'd finished reading.

"That's where I found it," said Dad. His smile exhibited pride and pleasure.

It's the artist in him, I suppose.

Harry owned a gas station two blocks from Oakland Avenue. Dad used to go over, sit by his desk in his small office, fill the air with his cigarette smoke and talk to Harry whenever there was a lull in Harry's business. Sometimes, he stayed for hours. Harry was one of those people who thought a lot of him. Dad was a good conversationalist; most people who knew him seemed to like him.

I loved Harry. I could tell he'd been a handsome young man. His effervescent smile greeted me before he ever spoke a word. Harry had the perfectly shaped head and face for a man who was completely bald.

Whenever he saw me—and right up until I left Welland—he always asked, "How's my girl, today?" He and his wife, Margery, had two grown-up boys by the time our family moved to Welland. They no longer had children living with them. I thought they must be lonely for some kid company.

Sometimes, in the early evening after supper, I would knock on their door, be invited in and then just sit and visit with them. Margery would offer me home-baked cookies, a piece of lemon cake or, occasionally, a piece of her cherry pie—my favourite. I would sit and eat while they asked me about my day. Eagerly, I shared my news with them. I never met a kinder couple than Harry and Margery. They insisted I call them by their first names. I used to think what a fine father Harry would be to a daughter.

As I was reminiscing, the car had been getting chilly. I looked toward the front door. There stood Mom. Her breath had created a haze on the glass. It was almost eerie. Her face appeared like an apparition.

Someday, you'll die, Mom. How I'll miss you, when God takes you to be with him!

I tucked my grey and maroon scarf into my black leather coat, opened the car door and stuck my boot into a pile of snow. I shook off the clumps, walked around the car and headed toward the house.

The sidewalk had been shovelled by the teenage boy who lived two houses over from Mom and Dad. Five steps above the walk, Mom held the door open for me. The aroma of her triple-chocolate cake wafted through the opening. I peered around Mom toward the kitchen.

My taste buds had been alerted and were ready to receive her offering of cake and a cup of tea.

After I had spoken with Shirley on Tuesday, I called Mom to let her know I was coming for an overnight visit. I wanted to give her something to look forward to—to cushion the impact of the impending news of her move.

Before I removed my boots and coat, my mother's arms surrounded me. It felt good. I kissed her soft, rouged cheek.

As Mom and I proceeded to the living room, I heard a car door slam. Mom returned to the front door. Dad was sitting with his legs extended over the furnace grate. He wore a burgundy bathrobe with blue flannel pyjamas underneath. Thick grey wool socks were pulled up and over his pyjama bottoms. He appeared to be content and comfortable, as he sat quietly staring at the grate.

I kissed the top of Dad's head. Even though Dad's hair had thinned considerably, fine white and black strands still streaked back from his high forehead. Mom had finally influenced him with respect to cleanliness. When I came close to him, I inhaled the scent of shaving cream. For years, he would use a straight razor every other day—sometimes not even that often. Now, he looked and smelled like a dignified elderly gentleman: clean-shaven and well-scrubbed!

Hmmm…Irish Spring.

Dad looked up, "Is that Shirley I hear, Claudia?" he asked.

"It's me, Dad," Shirley answered as she walked toward the living room from the hallway.

Dad moved his legs back for Mom and Shirley as they came into the room. I sat across from him in Grandma Philp's rocking chair.

"How about that Claude—having two of our girls visiting at the same time." Mom's smile radiated her delight.

Dad nodded and gave a half-smile.

He knows he and Mom will have short notice with respect to their move from the house. With a network of people from the Bible study and my friends praying for the transition, I trust that any challenges will be handled wisely.

Our afternoon was spent sitting around the dining room table chatting—all of us eating chocolate cake with scoops of vanilla ice cream and drinking pots of tea.

It was Shirley who broke the news to our parents.

"Mom, Dad—you're probably wondering why we're here for an overnight."

"Uh-huh," said Mom—her smile vanished. "I've been thinking about it."

"I got a call yesterday from Sunset Haven and a room has become available for you and Dad. You'll be moving tomorrow. Claudia and I are here to help you pack your suitcases and drive you over.

"I knew—I had a feeling...." Mom's voice trailed off.

"I don't want to leave," said Dad, as he looked past my mother to the portrait he had done of Grandma Philp.

I was sitting beside him at the table. I picked up my spoon and began stirring in my near empty tea cup.

"Dad," I said, "tomorrow morning, I'm going to take you to the shoe store and buy you a new pair of Romeos. Your big toe on your right foot is wearing through your leather slippers—you need a new pair. Would you like that, Dad?"

The one material object Dad was attached to was his Romeo slippers. Mom had purchased a pair of the soft leather slippers for him as a Christmas present, several years before.

"It's important for your feet and back to have a well-made pair of shoes and slippers to walk in, Claude," I imagined her telling him.

Dad's face lit up, "Okay! Tomorrow morning, before we move?"

"Uh-huh...first thing after breakfast. Your feet will be comfy and you'll look spiffy to boot!"

"Yar."

I felt relieved.

"Violet asked me not long ago what I was going to do the day I move," said Mom. "I told her, 'My children are taking care of everything. I'm going to walk out of the door, lock it and leave.'"

The following day went as planned. Dad and I enjoyed eating our breakfast of poached eggs on toast and shopping for his Romeos.

Mom stayed at the house while she and Shirley packed the suitcases.

Dad and I did something we had never done before as adults: we spent the morning together, just the two of us. I felt our relationship had come full circle, only this time, I was giving back to Dad what I'd received from him as a little girl: love.

Thank you, Lord.

35

Complications

The LORD is my strength and my shield; my heart trusts in
him, and I am helped (Psalm 28:7).

1989 was working itself up to a slow boil. It had started out well
enough with Mom and Dad easing nicely into their routine at
Sunset Haven. Their room on the second floor was spacious and
bright. Although all of their framed photographs of their grandchildren had not yet been brought to their new home, Shirley and
I had taken their three large photograph albums with us when we
moved them in. Photos had always been important to Mom and
Dad. We often looked through them when visiting—remembering
some of the more enjoyable times with family.

Later, I had a chance to look at the letters in Dad's correspondence album. As I had only the responses from those with whom
he had corresponded, I could only guess what the nature of Dad's
own letters had been.

Here is one from his family doctor:

Dr. Ian MacDonald
May 25, 1953
Dear Mr. Philp,
Thank you for your letter of May 3. It reached me just before
I was leaving for a short trip—it gave me such satisfaction

and pleasure that the trip was doubly enjoyable. Pardon the delay in replying.

It is good to know that you have work which you can like and which can provide an outlet for your imagination and liking for people. I would make one suggestion, that is, don't go at it too strenuously at first. Let a few roots take hold before letting the trunk get too big.

The news of your father was a bit sad, but it did seem to strengthen my opinion that you personally need have no fear of mental disturbance. With that horror laid to rest, it should be much easier for you to bear up under the burden of discomfort which you—like all of us in lesser degrees must bear from time to time.

Have you learned to live in daylight compartments? And have you accepted the fact that if each of us does his best, no one will expect us to do more?

Let me know how things go. In the meantime, best wishes.

Sincerely,

Ian MacDonald

This letter left me puzzled as to what had transpired in conversation between Dr. MacDonald and Dad. What had he told the doctor regarding Grandpa Philp and his own fears of being like him? How could the doctor possibly know that Dad "need have no fear of mental disturbance"? I wondered how truthful my father had been in what he told Dr. MacDonald. He had a sympathetic ear in the doctor.

Daylight compartments?

Will I ever fully know my father?

★ ★ ★ ★ ★

After Mom and Dad moved into Sunset Haven, the house on Oakland Avenue was put on the market and sold within a month.

The money from the trust fund Chuck had established for my parents enabled the purchase of new furniture for the large, rectangular room my parents now shared on the Haven's second floor. My mother had been tickled with the purchases. Chuck and I went with her, and she gave us the nod when she found what she thought would be complementary colours to go with the curtains in the room. Light rose-coloured winged back chairs, were purchased along with a matching area rug that covered approximately 100 square feet in the space allotted for Mom and Dad's living room. Their twin beds, at the back of the room, were placed side by side with nightstands and lamps provided for each of them.

How odd it was to see them share a room after over thirty years of sleeping apart. Somehow, I felt it gave comfort to both of them to be together in what they knew would be their last home.

Mom and Dad had been living at Sunset Haven for one week when I paid my first visit.

January 27, 1989
Before Chuck left on a business trip to Europe this morning, we prayed together. I prayed God would give me another opportunity to speak further to Dad about faith. I spent from 11 a.m. until 7:30 p.m. with Mom and Dad.

After our dinner in the cafeteria, we went back to their room at 6:00 p.m. I read 2 Corinthians 4. We then proceeded to pray. I spoke with Mom and Dad until 7:30. Dad told me his father had turned him away from religion. We discussed that for a while. I felt very good when I left. I think it brought Mom and Dad comfort.

* * * * *

February 16, 1989
A week ago Tuesday, for the first time, I gave my personal testimony at a local church. Things have been going badly ever since. My neighbour, Isobel Wassink, said yesterday, "The closer we are to God the more the enemy tries to come between us." It seems to be true, for we are going through a terrible trial with Craig. I spent the entire evening on the phone last night, speaking with Shirley (who is in Florida), Carl and Trisha. Craig moved back into Mom and Dad's house and because he absolutely hates Chuck, told Carl he will fight Chuck every step of the way with respect to the house. Of course, Craig has no hope of succeeding. I see this entire affair getting very ugly.

Craig had moved to Winnipeg, but after several months decided to come back. By 1989, when Mom and Dad moved into Sunset Haven, none of us, other than Mom and Dad, had seen or heard from Craig for almost two years. He found out that Mom and Dad had moved to Sunset Haven and the house had been sold. Craig's skewed perspective regarding the ownership of Mom and Dad's house caused him to be suspicious of Chuck. Craig didn't seem to understand—or he chose to ignore—the fact that Chuck had helped Mom and Dad stay in their home an additional sixteen years. Although Craig knew the ownership of the house changed years ago and that it had been sold by Chuck, he decided to stop the sale by taking possession of the house.

When he came back from Winnipeg, he broke into the house on Oakland Avenue and moved in. Chuck was concerned the sale would not go through so he called Carl to help him deal with Craig. Carl agreed to meet Chuck in Welland to talk to Craig. They hoped Craig would be reasonable once he was told the house was sold and new owners would be moving in.

★ ★ ★ ★ ★

Chuck's cell phone rang during our drive to Welland around 11:00 a.m. the following day.

"Mom, what's wrong?" I looked over at Chuck. He tightened his grip on the wheel.

"What...what?" I said.

Chuck looked over at me, shook his head and held up his hand for me to keep quiet.

"We'll be there shortly—in about twenty minutes, Mom," said Chuck.

When the call ended, Chuck reached over and touched my arm.

"Craig went to Sunset Haven this morning, blew up at Mom, Dad and the staff and then left. He tried to persuade your parents to leave and go back with him to live in the house. When Mom told him, 'No,' he started to yell and curse. Your mother sounded shaky. Carl has been notified by the nursing staff, and he's on his way."

By the time we arrived at Sunset Haven, Carl was there. The nurses managed to calm Mom. Dad was lying on his bed with his eyes closed. When we began to speak, he looked up at us and slowly brought his feet to the floor and stared into space.

I put my arm around him as I sat down. Dad grasped the side of the bed with his hands, leaned forward and began to rock back and forth. I dropped my hand from his shoulder as he began to speak.

"Craig...he put his face down to mine and starting swearing at me as I lay on my bed. Your mother came up behind him and asked him to leave me alone. He turned and started to yell at her. He wanted us to pack and go back to the house."

"It's okay, Dad." I put my hand over his. "The guys are going to handle this."

Mom stood between Chuck and Carl. She continued to pick at the clump of tissue clenched in her hand.

"Craig's mentally ill," she said, her eyes two pools of tears. "He needs help, he needs to go to the hospital."

"We'll take care of this, Mom," said Chuck. "Claudia will stay with you and Dad while Carl and I go to the police station. We won't go into the house with just the two of us. I think we need to be careful with Craig."

At the police station, Carl and Chuck explained what happened at the nursing home earlier that morning. They also explained Craig had broken into the house and was living there without permission. Craig's actions convinced them that three officers should accompany my husband and brother to the house.

With lights flashing, two cruisers followed Carl and Chuck down the quiet residential street of Oakland Avenue.

In the meantime, while I stayed with Mom and Dad, I convinced them to come home for a visit with Chuck and me. I felt being with my family and having the enjoyment of Melinda and Cameron's company would divert their thoughts and maybe help them to heal somewhat from the shock of Craig's behaviour.

When Chuck and Carl returned to Sunset Haven, they told us Craig had been admitted to the psychiatric wing of the hospital.

"Mom," said Carl, "we told Craig you thought he should go to the hospital. He went willingly."

★ ★ ★ ★ ★

When Mom and Dad were settled in our guest room for the night, Chuck and I sat side by side against the headboard in our bedroom as he described what had taken place with Craig.

"We pulled up to the sidewalk in front of the house. All of the curtains were drawn. The officer in the cruiser in front of us opened his car door, stood and waited for Carl and me. The three of us walked together toward the house. The sidewalk was packed down with snow. We walked up the icy steps to the front door, but before we had a chance to knock, the door opened. Out came Craig with his hands up in the air. He said, 'I surrender.' Then, he walked down the steps with his hands still in the air, mumbling stuff I couldn't understand."

"When I first saw him, I saw how much he had changed. He'd grown a beard. His stomach was hanging over his jeans; his eyes had a wild look about them. He walked right by us—eyes straight ahead. As he walked with the police officer toward the cruiser, I noticed he wasn't wearing any shoes—only socks. He seemed oblivious to the cold and snow. Carl went back into the house to get his boots, but Craig kept on walking. The police officer opened the back door for him and he slid into the seat."

"Carl signed the admission form when we arrived at the hospital. Craig was admitted to the psychiatric ward, but didn't say a word to us—just continued muttering to himself."

"After we left the hospital, we drove back to the house. The kitchen window was boarded up and all of the curtains were drawn. He had smashed every framed family portrait that hung on the walls. There was glass all over the place."

"You mean even the ones of the grandchildren?" I slunk down on my pillow and stared at Shirley's oil painting on the wall across from our bed. *Beautiful.* My eyes rested on the deep vivid blue hydrangeas. It somehow kept me from sobbing.

"All of them." Chuck reached over and took my left hand in his. It felt warm and protective. "We cleaned everything up."

I pictured the face of each of Mom and Dad's twelve grandchildren—smiling faces that greeted them each morning as they walked down the stairs. *Photographs on the dining room walls, in the hallways, in each of the three bedrooms—all smashed...*

★ ★ ★ ★ ★

Chuck called the hospital the following day and was told Craig had left. No further information was given.

Although he had earlier broken into the house by smashing a window, we had the locks changed on the house to prevent Craig from returning. We counted on the fact Craig would be unnerved by the police's recent involvement.

Mom and Dad stayed with us for a week. By the time they returned to Sunset Haven, they seemed refreshed and relaxed. We never mentioned that Craig checked himself out of the hospital.

The staff at Sunset Haven were alerted to be on the lookout if Craig ever returned to the nursing home.

36

Experiencing God

Create in me a pure heart, O God, and renew a steadfast spirit within me (Psalm 51:10, NIV).

1989

The decision was made. I would visit Mom and Dad every Thursday. My alarm was set for 6:00 a.m. which enabled me to reach Welland by 7:45 a.m. It was the one day of the week when Holy Trinity Church held communion at 8:00 a.m. I knew Mom wouldn't be able to go to church on Sundays, as there was no one to take her.

For years after her retirement from Mitchell's Ladies' Wear, Mom had volunteered at the church. I'm not sure what her role was during her time of volunteering, but in conversation with Mom, I witnessed her moving closer to the Lord. As I glanced through her Bible, I noticed pieces of paper between its pages with written personal prayers and Scripture verses.

Thursdays meant a great deal to me. I even looked forward to the drive. I would slip a tape into the cassette player of my car radio, and whoosh down the driveway singing along with my favorite hymns from *Majesty and Glory*. I listened to the music in its entirety, and this seemed to set me on a spiritual level whereby I eased into my prayer time. All the while, I sensed the presence of the Holy Spirit. As the drive took approximately 90 minutes, I would pray for about an hour and then listen to WDCX—the Christian radio station out of Buffalo, New York.

When I arrived at 7:45 a.m., Mom would be ready to leave for the ten minute drive to the church. She would be impeccably dressed in her light wool, teal green, straight skirt, partnered with her grey sweater and her blue, green and grey wool jacket.

As I entered their room on one such Thursday, I could see Dad stretched out on top of his bed. His maroon housecoat almost covering his blue-and-white striped, flannel pyjamas.

Someone must have shaved him.

After giving Mom a hug, I went over to Dad's bed.

"Good-bye, Dad. See you after church. Sure you don't want to come with us?" I asked, knowing full well his answer.

He didn't respond.

"Okay...we'll go out for lunch when we get back and have some ice cream for dessert."

Without looking up or opening his eyes, he said, "That'll be nice, Claudia."

I leaned over and kissed his gaunt face, inhaling the fragrance of Old Spice aftershave. As I lingered there for a moment, Dad opened his eyes, smiled at me and closed them again.

"See you in an hour and a half, Dad."

June 23, 1989
Every Thursday when I visit with Mom and Dad, I do a Bible study with them for an hour or more. [Mostly, I read Scripture and we discussed it.] Dad seems to enjoy this time together. Last night when we sat down for dinner in the cafeteria, he asked Mom if she was going to pray. Whenever Dad goes out with Mom for a drive or shopping, I put on the Majesty *and* Glory *tape. Dad recognizes many of the hymns. He sometimes sings along. It's encouraging to see the steps toward faith that he seems to be making.*

July 14, 1989
Remarkable things have been occurring lately. Dad went to church last week for the first time in years. He even prayed the Lord's Prayer with the congregation. Two weeks ago, Aunt Dorothy (who

*also lives in Sunset Haven) joined us for Bible study and sat lis-
tening intently while I read.*

My Dad's younger sister had been a woman of faith just as my
Grandma Philp had been. When I had first read my grandmother's
diary from 1933, there were many notations about Aunt Dorothy
and Grandpa Philp going to the East End Mission together.
According to the diary entries of Grandma Philp, Aunt Olive, who
was a few years younger than Aunt Dorothy, appeared to have an
unnamed malady. Hence the reason, I suppose, that Grandma
stayed home with Aunt Olive while Aunt Dorothy attended
church with my grandfather.

★ ★ ★ ★ ★

May 16, 1989
*Sally Gleason has asked me to help her with a three-day confer-
ence for Reformed women to be held in May 1990. She wants me
to do a 1 ½ hour seminar on devotions and also to open each session.
I would love to do it for her and the Lord, especially. God seems to
be leading me where I have yet to see I have talent. I can't imagine
holding an audience captive for an hour and a half. God wouldn't
lead me to where I don't belong. He hasn't so far. I will pray and
trust Him to use me as He will! It's crazy how I want to do it but
feel so inadequate—God must completely fill me here.*

May 29, 1989
*I spoke for the first time for Christian Women's Club tonight.
Melinda came with me, as did Gertrude Reed, my friend from the
Crisis Pregnancy Centre. I enjoyed the evening but moaned to
Melinda, afterward, about the fact that the chairman didn't give
any response to my testimony of faith. I felt down about it; even
though many encouraging things were said to me by others.*
    *When I talked to Chuck this evening he said, "Who were you
doing this for—yourself or for God? Because, it sounds to me like
you were more interested in getting the glory."*

Ouch. Of course he was right!

* * * * *

July 14, 1989

I have begun working on the seminar I have been asked to lead next May. The topic will be on the Christian's devotional life. I've started preparing an outline—looking forward to it. I pray God will guide me and use me to bring women into a closer relationship with Him.

For a while now, I have been keeping a journal and noting where God has guided me in various circumstances. At the Crisis Pregnancy Centre, the other day, I spent three hours counselling a 21-year-old woman who had many problems. She said she knew God but had been straddling the line with respect to her commitment. She is having an affair with a married man so we got into a heavy discussion. I prayed with her before she left. I felt God's leading throughout the entire session. I believed he had given me the wisdom to say the right things to her. She was receptive to listening; although, she told me she remained confused. I'll never know the outcome of our meeting but felt I was making progress as I was led by the Holy Spirit.

True wisdom comes from God, I've learned through reading the Bible. Complete dependence on that fact gives me confidence when I speak for Christian Women's Club; or when I'm at the Crisis Pregnancy Centre. I know it is not something I possess on my own but rather the courage God gives to me as I honour him.

"I am the vine, you are the branches. If a man remains in me and I in him, he will bear much fruit; apart from me you can do nothing. If anyone does not remain in me, he is like a branch that is thrown away and withers; such branches are picked up, thrown into the fire and burned. If you remain in me and my words remain you, ask whatever you wish, and it will be given you. This is to my Father's glory that you bear much fruit, showing yourselves to be my disciples" (John 15:5-7, NIV)

July 21, 1989

Thank you, God, for all you're doing in the life of my father! He went to church again on Thursday. In the evening, when we did Bible study, Mom said he didn't take his eyes off me—he really listened. I do believe my prayers are being answered and that Dad is being drawn closer to you. It's exciting to witness. Aunt Dorothy joined us again and everyone was quite chatty after we had finished.

We stayed together for two hours: doing our study and then talking. I think it's such a wonderful gift God has given all of us by enabling the study as well as our prayer time together. Dad had requested that I pray for him to sleep. When I phoned yesterday, he told me he had slept through the night.

Had this occurrence convinced Dad God cared for him? Ever since I could remember, Dad had trouble sleeping. When I would go to bed at night and then get up the next day, he would often have spent the night sleeping on the couch in the living room. If he fell asleep, he didn't want to become fully awake by having to go upstairs, change into his pyjamas and get into bed. On many nights, he slept in his clothes on the chesterfield.

August 15, 1989

Something I seem to be discovering: when people belong to God, their time no longer belongs to them. It's something that shouldn't be fought—only the desire to do what we want to do must be fought. He is at the helm and commands our undivided attention. Believers need to be all God wants them to be with each and every person God puts on their path. If Christians succumb to Him on all levels, the time and timing will be cherished. Believers must comfort those who call upon them and those who desire to be in their company. Often, God has put us with those whom we are in contact with for a purpose.

October 6, 1989

I am still experiencing an indescribable time with my mother on Thursdays. It's the highlight of each week. I will forever be indebted to God for allowing me this exceptional time. God's presence is felt when we are together. Mom never hesitates to tell me how much she has enjoyed our day.

Dad was sick with a chest infection and didn't join us but remained in bed for most of Thursday. His eyelids drooped. Moisture from his runny eyes spilled to his cheeks. Dad continually blew his nose with a Kleenex and patted his face with his handkerchief.

Mom and I went to church on our own. In the afternoon, we met Shirley for lunch. After visiting with Shirley, we went shopping at the Tammy Shop in Welland. Later in the day, I took Mom to the Casa del Toro for supper. It was such a pleasure to watch her smile and clap her hands with delight. We talked about the Lord and prayed for Craig before our meal. Mom wants to visit him but has promised me she won't attempt to do so alone. "I know you can't take me, Claudia. Maybe Carl will," she said. Mom was aware of Craig's contempt for me.

When I left Mom at Sunset Haven, she was appreciative of the time we had together. It was truly precious.

I put in a tape and listened to hymns on my journey home. While driving, I experienced the blessings of God. I felt exhilarated.

The Bible speaks of having the joy of the Lord. I believe my experiences reflect the happiness one has through faith in Christ. I had never known such a feeling. Sometimes, still, I feel a flutter like tiny angel wings in my stomach.

37

Trusting

But let all who take refuge in you be glad; let them ever sing for joy. Spread your protection over them, that those who love your name may rejoice in you (Psalm 5:11, NIV).

Being an emotionally charged individual, and still young in my relationship with Christ, I needed to learn to not always trust my feelings to govern me. With respect to Dad, he still had the ability to affect my responses to his behaviour. I came to doubt his conversations regarding faith had been real because at times he would still act like the person I had long known him to be—only without the influence of alcohol.

August 21, 1990
Transcending all barriers of resistance, I felt God had worked his miraculous powers upon Dad today. He was in good spirits when I arrived at Sunset Haven. We went down for coffee and then out for lunch. Dad spent the entire day with Mom and me. He was re-markably alert and spoke with me more than he has for many months. He even went to see Aunt Olive [who was in a secure ward in the same facility] *and managed to remain non-reactive to the surrounding people calling out such things as, "I want to go home." "Where's my mommy?" Many had the symptoms of de-mentia.* [Aunt Olive was also now suffering with this disease.]

I have never witnessed Dad being so agreeable.

After visiting with Aunt Olive, we went upstairs to read the Bible. Dad told me how he had recently looked up the passage in John 13:5 where Jesus washed the feet of the disciples. "After that, he poured water into a basin and began to wash his disciples' feet, drying them with the towel that was wrapped around him."

"Isn't that something—Jesus washing someone's feet?" Dad remarked. "It was an act of humility."

"I had a talk with a Jew, once," Dad continued. "He didn't believe Jesus was the Messiah. He thought he was just a great scholar and teacher."

We also spoke about Jesus' saying, "My God, my God why hast thou forsaken me?" Dad couldn't understand why Jesus would say that if he were God.

I explained that the human aspect of Jesus' character required him to suffer. As well as suffering on the cross, Jesus suffered emotionally through a period of separation from God. He took on our sin so we may be forgiven and have eternal life.

September 3, 1990
Today is the first time Craig will be visiting Mom and Dad since last July when he went berserk at Sunset Haven. I've prayed for reconciliation. I requested that he return only in love. He has asked forgiveness for what he had done. He said, in a note Mom had shown me, "I wasn't myself." I pray Craig will turn to God and that he will depart from his life of perversion. I will never give up on this prayer for him. I also pray that Dad will be comfortable in Craig's presence. I'm leaving all at the feet of Jesus.

November 8, 1990
I believe God transcended all human barriers and threw aside the enemy's grip on Dad, today. I saw a visible transformation occur in him which I have never seen before. Mom told me Dad was having a very bad morning. This had upset her. We went to the dining room where he was sitting. He looked like he had been pulled through a knothole. He was pale and unshaven. His eyes were puffy, his lips curved downward and he sat slumped in the

chair. He was babbling to himself—nothing I could understand. At one point, he looked up at me and said, 'I'm going through hell.' I believed him. His appearance gave evidence of it. I decided to take Mom out for lunch after I'd waited for Dad to finish his. When we went back up to their room, he told me he would continue to go through hell because we were going to leave him. When I asked to him to come along, he refused. He kept repeating "each day I die" and then lay down on his bed. I went over to him, while Mom was in the washroom across the hall, and asked him why he felt so bad. He said "Because I'm going to hell." I asked him why he thought that. His response—"The devil told me."

I then asked him some questions.

"Do you believe God created heaven and earth?"

"Yes," he responded.

"Did God have a son named Jesus?"

"Yes."

"Did Jesus die on the cross to save us from eternal death, and do you believe it?"

"Yes."

"Dad, have you asked God to forgive your sins?"

"Yes," Dad said in a loud and clear voice.

"It means, then, that you'll be going to heaven."

I had memorized John 14:1–3 and recited it for him. Never had I witnessed such a dramatic change in him. All of his anxiety seemed to have been dispelled.

We continued to talk until Mom came back into the room. By that time, he asked me if I thought it would be a good idea if he came with us.

"I love you, Dad, and want you to come along."

He suggested he sit in the back seat so Mom could be in the front with me. I bought him an ice cream cone while Mom and I had lunch at a local restaurant. I felt so warm toward him (even though he kind of smelled and hadn't been shaved for a couple of days). It gave me much pleasure to see him enjoying the simple pleasure of eating his ice cream cone.

While Mom and I went into the mall, Dad sat in the car listening to a praise tape I had put in for him. When we returned, a half an hour later, he remarked how much he liked listening to the tape *because many of the hymns were familiar to him.*

When I told him I had bought him bananas, he said, 'Thank you, God bless you, Claudia.'

Wow!

We had such a great afternoon. Dad was so different, I could scarcely believe my ears and eyes because he not only sounded good but was beginning to look good underneath all his whiskers. (He still didn't smell too good, though.)

After a nice dinner together, later on that day, we went back to the room. As I was about to leave for the washroom, Dad said, "I hate to see you go."

"Gee, Dad, you don't usually seem to mind." His mouth fell open. "I love you very much," he said. I gave him a hug and kiss and told him I also loved him.

As I left for the washroom, I told Dad and Mom I would read the Bible when I returned. I handed Dad an old copy from 1988 of 'Our Daily Bread' [a devotional]. When I returned, Dad had the page open to include verses from 2 Cor. 5 [regarding our heavenly dwelling]. It had been very appropriate concerning what we could anticipate in the life hereafter.

When I asked if he had any prayer requests, he told me to pray for Uncle Harry (Mom's younger brother) who was in the hospital. Also, he asked for prayer for his lost false teeth and that the head-ache he'd had earlier in the day would not return.

We prayed for Craig's salvation and his visit, for Dad's anxiety and the enemy's silence from making Dad believe he was going to go to hell.

Dad had radiated happiness most of the day. It was truly a testimony of God's presence in his life.

We parted in joy and with peace. Mom was elated. This morning it had been quite the opposite feeling for her. I believe Mom and Dad had to go through this very difficult morning together. She had been distressed over Dad's behaviour, but then she'd witnessed God's supernatural power in his life and God's ability to transform Dad's attitude and behaviour.

To recognize the changes I witnessed in Dad was a strong encouragement. Still, there were times when I was left confused about him and his relationship with the Lord. I seemed to have difficulty understanding that God might not be removing the particular thorn of Dad's psychological problems from his side.

Was I the one whose faith was being tested regarding God's providential plan in the life of the believer? Had I left my past completely behind me without worry of falling into my old ways? I still had much to learn about God's grace and also about the struggles I personally would continue to grapple with until the day I would come face to face with God.

Why would it be any different for Dad?

★ ★ ★ ★ ★

When Craig tried to return to Sunset Haven for a visit in July 1990, Mom persuaded the staff to let him come into the residence. He apologized for his past behaviour and was allowed a short visit. The family later found out that the visit was, once again, about money.

Every resident of Sunset Haven had access to a small personal cash account kept at the front desk for incidentals: snacks at the coffee shop, shampoo, toiletries, etc. We were told by staff that Craig tried to get Mom to withdraw the balance that was in this account and give it to him. The staff was fairly quickly aware of his behaviour, and he was asked to leave. To my knowledge, Mom told Carl about it but never discussed it with me nor—as far as I know—with any other member of the family. Because Craig didn't get the money he wanted, Mom knew he wouldn't come back to see her and Dad.

★ ★ ★ ★ ★

Following his visit to the nursing home, Craig sent letters to Shirley and Chuck asking them to finance another film—this one, a horror movie. Craig knew Trisha and Carl could not afford what he was asking so he approached Chuck and Shirley. He stated he needed $10,000 "as soon as possible." These letters were sent ten days after he visited Mom and Dad.

As I read his letter to Chuck, the name Craig proposed for his movie caused me to shudder: *HAMMER, The Studio That Dripped*

BLOOD! He had done some graphics with the title—each brilliant red letter looked as though it was dripping with blood.

He was turned down by both Shirley and Chuck who suggested he seek psychological counselling.

Craig notified Chuck that he'd moved to Toronto in order to continue to collect the Trust's interest cheques.

38

Despair

"Come to me, all you who are weary and burdened, and I will give you rest. Take my yoke upon you and learn from me, for I am gentle and humble in heart, and you will find rest for your souls" (Matthew 11:28–29, NIV).

Although I had once clearly told Craig how I felt—that I cared about him no matter what lifestyle he chose to live—he wasn't satisfied. He wanted me to wholeheartedly embrace his choices. I, in turn, based on my reading of Scripture, began to give him my firm opinion of God's point of view. We grew further and further apart.

At one point, with the intention of making a movie on the gay lifestyle, Craig phoned me. During our conversation, he asked me, despite my beliefs, to accept a role in a movie he was going to make on the life of Ernie and Jim—two of his cohabiting gay friends. When I told him I couldn't be part of something I thought was wrong, he became angry and accused me of being homophobic. He raised his voice and began a tirade of abusive language.

Chuck walked into the kitchen and heard my side of the conversation. He got the gist of it. As he watched my face blanch and the tears fall, he took the receiver from my hand. Shaking, I left the room as he asked Craig about the conversation we were having. Chuck objected to what Craig was asking me to do.

"We care about you Craig, but we will not tell you that living the homosexual lifestyle is acceptable."

My brother hung up.

My journals became filled with Scripture verses. Some I had memorized—drawing on those that helped me through my loss but also those that kept me in constant intimacy with God. I prayed for him to keep me level-headed and focused as I continued to speak for Christian Women's Club about my faith journey.

However, one concern remained a constant: the fear that Craig would return to Sunset Haven.

I was told by staff that when Craig visited Mom and Dad the previous summer, he came in cursing and yelling at both the staff members and Mom and Dad. At that point, they were able to get assistance from other workers at the home to remove Craig. Subsequently, a court order was issued to prevent him from coming back into Sunset Haven.

Apparently, Craig wanted additional money from the sale of the house—money to which he said he was entitled. The reason for the visit was to work on Mom's sympathy. He wanted money out of the trust fund set up for Mom and Dad from the proceeds of the sale of the house.

This account had been set up for Mom and Dad. The money was to be used for their personal needs, including furnishings for their room. My mother wanted Craig to have the remainder of the trust fund after she and Dad were gone. They discussed this with Chuck who acted as their lawyer. In the meantime, it was arranged that Craig would receive interest from the capital in the Trust. But Craig wasn't satisfied with just the interest and was trying to manipulate them—using abusive language—to get what he wanted: money to finance the gay movie he was hoping to make.

39

"Good-bye"

God is our refuge and strength, an ever present help in trouble (Psalm 46:1, NIV).

We heard nothing more from Craig until April 29, 1991. He was after the money from Mom and Dad's trust fund again, and he was turned down. A letter followed in answer to my letter when I had told him, "No."

29, April 1991
Dear Claudia:
Chuck seems to think that I needed to reply to your letter dated March 28. I am taking up his suggestion at this time. Your correspondence does demand a response towards yourself. Please bear with me as I begin to relay my side of the story.

Realize my hatred and anger is a reaction to your hatred and anger. I feel my sister's complete contempt for my very existence. It's a problem you have with my being born, in my opinion. You had a real difficulty with jealousy and it has never been addressed.

Your husband has been the means by which you have been able to carry on your crusade of intolerance. Chuck has simply carried on your desire to control and punish. He treats me exactly the same way you treated me as a child! I will not be manipulated like some naïve and stupid sibling.

The Philp Family Trust has become outdated and outmoded in its usefulness. There needs to be a new agreement written up to accommodate my circumstances as well as other family members. I am willing to have my lawyer compose an agreement, allowing one-fifth of the trust fund to be transferred to me.

Both you and your husband have stated flat out that taking any risks in production [of the movie] are out of the question. You leave me no alternative but to respectfully demand my one-fifth share. The interest of course will not be coming my way.

Sincerely yours,
Craig Philp

Craig wrote a further letter to Chuck:

May 10, 1991
Dear Sir:
I've received your letter dated May 9, 1991. Please be advised that I no longer wish to receive anything from my family. I want no interest. The family can keep it for themselves. I understand that the trust was set up for my parents as well as myself.

I'm sick and tired of being labelled "selfish" by Claudia. You make me sick to my stomach. What else can I say? I have no parents. I have no siblings. It doesn't make sense to send me money from strangers. You keep saying to me that there is only one way to live and you have it.

Claude Jesse and Dora Gertrude are no longer my parents. They can adopt you if they wish! If you send me any money, I will return it to your office! Do I make myself absolutely clear?

It's not worth it for me to take legal action to get what I want. Keep the money. Keep the property. Keep your values. You have your life to live and I have mine. As my one time friend Gerry Culig said about me [sic], "Claudia is so full of sh*t with her religion that to have anything to do with her is destructive!"

Should I make a film entitled, "Homophobes from Hell"? The many adventures of the Philps. I am a *Rebel With a Cause*. You do not understand anything about me. This is the end of the show! I want no more letters, no more phone calls from the police or anyone else. [Craig had been calling our house about fifteen times a day and then hanging up. Before he moved from St. Catharines, where Shirley lived, he did this to her as well. When he moved back to Toronto, the phone calls to her house stopped and the calls to mine began. Once the police confronted him, the phone calls stopped.]

Good-bye my dear sweet siblings.

Sincerely,

Craig Michael Philp

Chuck continued to send him the interest from the trust fund; Craig continued to cash the cheques.

★ ★ ★ ★ ★

Although Craig was seldom spoken of once he severed ties from his family, the loss of my youngest brother left me grief stricken. Our formerly close relationship had exploded like a landmine, leaving its shrapnel of pain. On the one hand, I felt deep sorrow but on the other hand, I felt intense anger over his unmitigated attacks upon our family, particularly Mom and Dad. I only shared these feelings with Chuck.

As I continued to grow in my faith, I developed a clearer under-standing of God's perspective on Craig's lifestyle choices. Things I had read in the Bible prior to my conversion now became more clearly defined. Answers to hard questions helped me grasp some of the issues regarding Craig's behaviour and where it was taking him.

Like my older brother and two sisters, Craig was brought up in the church and attended Sunday school. He had also served as an altar boy. Did it mean nothing to him?

They may be ever seeing but never perceiving, and ever hear-ing but never understanding; otherwise they might turn and be forgiven (Mark 4:12).

Scripture was my constant refuge. God had become my Source of all comfort and truth. It was difficult to accept the futility of Craig's life and where he seemed to be headed. I stayed in God's Word on a daily basis. All of life's challenges brought me back to Scripture for the answers.

40

Separated

When answers to our prayers do not come at once, we should combine quiet patience and joyful confidence in our perservering prayer.[31]

February 13, 1992
I have been praying that my father, once again, repeatedly saying he is going to hell, will receive assurance from God about his salvation. Dad didn't appear to be all that good when I arrived today. He kept asking me to kiss him. I complied but he remained agitated —pacing back and forth in the room.

I wondered if my Bible reading and praying with Dad had been making him insecure about my feelings for him. Was he trying to win my favour by saying he believed when he actually didn't?

Today when I spoke to the Unit Manager, Carolyn Cronin, she told me the time had come to move Mom and Dad—they required much more care and supervision. Dad was incontinent and had to wear an adult diaper. Unfortunately, they will have to move both him and Mom as soon as a room becomes available.
When I was about to leave today, Dad (who had become lucid and calm) looked at me and said, 'I'm not going to go to hell and I know that now.' His face was relaxed; his eyes clear. I asked him,

"How do you know that now, Dad?" "Because I feel it inside," came his response.

We read Scripture together and prayed. Afterward, Mom and Dad walked me to the door of their room. When I said "good-bye" to them, I watched them walk back into their room. About to get into the car, I looked up at their second floor window where both Mom and Dad stood waving at me. A feeling of comfort washed over me. As I began my drive home, I slipped in the Majesty and Glory *tape.*

★ ★ ★ ★ ★

Mom and Dad, after sixty-five years of marriage, were removed from their spacious, sun-filled room—the room they had learned to call home.

Dad was taken to another area of the nursing home where he had to share a room with a stranger. Mom remained in the same section of the home, but was also moved into a room she had to share with someone unknown to her. Mom didn't seem to be aware of the change. Unless I raised it, she never mentioned Dad, at least not in my presence.

41

God with us

Dear friends, do not be surprised at the painful trial you are suffering as though something strange were happening to you. But rejoice that you participate in the sufferings of Christ, so that you may be overjoyed when his glory is revealed (1 Peter 4:12–13, NIV).

During the decline in Mom's cognitive abilities, I found the verses in the letters of Peter began to guide my understanding.

The words seemed to epitomize Mom's life with Dad, including the pain of loss when Craig turned on her. I believe Mom knew the peace of God that transcends all understanding.[32] Without the ability to remember her past, Mom's disposition remained cheerful. When I visited her, she would often sing, "Onward Christian Soldiers"—obviously a favourite, or maybe just the song Mom could remember best in its entirety.

"Stop that racket!" Dad said one day when I took her to visit him in the men's section of Sunset Haven.

By this time, both Mom and Dad were confined to wheelchairs. They were too weak to walk anywhere on their own.

When Dad demanded Mom stop singing, I knelt down by her wheelchair and took her hand, "Mom, can you stop singing while we are visiting with Dad? It seems to bother him."

She appeared to understand and grew silent but about thirty

seconds later, she began singing again. Dad yelled again about the noise. I had her say, "Good-bye" to him, and we left the men's section and returned to her room.

It was sad to experience these changes, but it was to be expected. By this time in 1993, Mom was eighty-five years old and Dad was eighty eight.

I tried a few more times to take Mom for visits with him, but she continued to sing, and he continued to tell her to stop. To me, he appeared to be miserable every time we visited.

Mom and Dad seemed to accept their changes without a fuss, although Dad's sour moods may have been an indication of the pain he was suffering, both physically and psychologically. His doctor continued to prescribe anti-depressants for him which often made him appear dopey. The pain medication didn't always seem effective in relieving his discomfort. With respect to memory, Dad was still doing much better than Mom. He remembered everyone and could spell exceptionally well, although he had become quieter and sometimes a little naughty.

"Don't bend over, now," he said to one of the nurses as she was about to pick up something off the floor. Dad sat staring at the back of her—waiting for an opportunity to poke her with the tip of his slipper.

"Oh, oh," I raised my eyebrows when Shirley told me of the incident. "They'll catch on to him," I said.

Not being able to distance myself from the situation sufficiently to look at my Dad objectively, I grew discouraged, believing all our discussions, including the Bible studies Dad had participated in, had been for nought. I had forgiven him and grown to love him, but I still did not fully trust him. I remained skeptical regarding the sincerity of his faith.

Do I still not know my father?

I felt his change should have been complete and manifested in an obvious way. What did this poor man have to do to make me believe he was saved? Nothing, I was to realize. It was something I needed to leave solely between God and Dad.

42

The man on the street

"He who is not with me is against me, and he who does not gather with me, scatters" (Luke 11:23, NIV).

1994

Following her bridal shower, Melinda and I circled the downtown Toronto block a second time as we headed for our home in Kettleby. It was 1994—one month before Melinda's May wedding.

"You don't really think that guy lying on the sidewalk under that grungy blanket is Uncle Craig, do you?" she asked.

I shrugged my shoulders as I slowly drove past the man whose body faced the street. He had hair like Craig—muddy brown and wiry. A thick growth of beard covered his face. Similar to Craig's beard, it had a tinge of red in it.

I glanced at my daughter and thought about the secrets that were kept within my family as I was growing up. I was determined not to allow history to repeat itself with respect to my own children. Melinda and Cameron were told about the hardships in the home where I was raised. As Melinda and I continued driving around the block, I turned toward her. "I don't know. It could be Craig. I just want to check the guy out," I said.

"But what if it is Uncle Craig? What will you do? Will you stop the car and go talk to him?"

"Probably not. What would I say?"

"I don't think it's him," said Melinda, sinking lower into her seat. "I hope not."

Turning the corner again, I checked the man lying on the street. I drew in a deep breath and exhaled a sigh of relief. It wasn't Craig.

★ ★ ★ ★ ★

On an evening in December that same year, our friends Ron and Sally Gleason said good-night to Chuck and me, as we parted company at Roy Thomson Hall in downtown Toronto. It was a tradition for the four of us to attend the Mendelssohn Choir performance of *Messiah* prior to Christmas.

The roads were covered in slush. It was a clear winter's night as we travelled west on the Gardiner Expressway toward home. Our conversation was interrupted by the ringing of Chuck's cellphone. I picked it up and handed it to him.

"Yes, this is Chuck speaking."

Pause.

"You tell Craig I'll be more than willing to help him if he's changed his attitude toward the family."

Silence.

"Okay, get back to me then." Chuck hung up and glanced at me. I waited for him to speak.

"That was a friend of Craig's. Craig's in jail. He was contacted by the police and wondered if I could help him. He said he hasn't seen Craig in years and doesn't know why the police called him."

As I processed the information, I felt indifferent—calm, emotionally detached—not as distraught as I used to be when reacting to disturbing news.

"I agree with what you told his friend. Craig's attitude needs to change toward our family."

"I don't think we'll hear back from him. I'll be surprised if we do."

"Me too."

It was the last time we were to hear news of Craig, who would never see Mom and Dad again.

43

No more sorrow

And we know that in all things God works for the good of those who love him, who have been called according to his purpose (Romans 8:28, NIV).

1995
Mom had become a gentle whisper of her former self. She continued to slip into the sinkhole of dementia until it swallowed up the last vestiges of her memory.

I stopped taking her to church on Thursdays as it became a challenge for her to get much out of it. Even though no more than twelve to fifteen people attended the service, Mom would get agitated.

"Why—who—all of them...?" Mom's voice trailed off as she spoke and waved her hand in the air.

While she groped for words, I tried to understand what she was attempting to say—careful not to upset her by giving correction.

"What's the matter with me, Claudie?" she whimpered, as she pulled at her ear.

There was no hiding it from her. She was aware of her increasing forgetfulness.

"Mom, we are still able to do lots together—you are physically healthy; we go out every week. Try not to worry about it. Sometimes, it's good to sit quietly together and enjoy the places we go."

"The good Lord, the good Lord...," Mom said as we took a drive through the rolling hills of Effingham, just outside St. Catharines. Mom looked out the window and pointed toward the clouds. "He did all this—all of this," she said.

"God, Mom?"

"Yes, God."

Mom had gradually become confused regarding the identity of family members and incoherent in her conversations—sentences were often disjointed.

While I kept Thursdays as my day of the week to visit with Mom and Dad, I changed the things we did together. I began to bring in photograph albums. We sat on her bed and looked through them. Dad was never interested.

"That's a cute boy," Mom said as she pointed at a black and white photo of Craig taken when he was about four years old. She briefly examined it, then turned the page.

One of the areas of my faith where I felt challenged was with the fact Mom had had such a difficult life, and now her youngest son had turned his back on her. It was an unremitting sorrow for her for the first two years she lived in Sunset Haven. *Why would God allow this to happen?*

Eventually, there came a time when she no longer mentioned Craig's name.

As I meditated on Romans 8:28, I began to see that Mom, in her increasing dementia, was being released from the torment she felt over the loss of Craig. I began to understand that in this circumstance, Mom was being protected from the misery she felt when Craig turned on her and the family. It seemed God was using Mom's debilitating disease to obliterate her awareness of the sorrow of her loss. And, Mom still had much to give to others with her ever-present joy and cheerfulness.

44

"Good-bye, Mom"

Blessed is the one who perseveres under trial because, having stood the test, that person will receive the crown of life that the Lord has promised to those who love him (James 1:12, NIV).

1995
Her head slowly moved in my direction as I held a spoonful of vanilla pudding ready to slip into her mouth. Lunch was almost over and Mom hadn't spoken a word.

After the last spoonful, she looked into my eyes, smiled obliquely and said, "Love."

"Love, Mom—I love you, too." I put the spoon back into the bowl and wrapped my arms around her shoulders. My mother continued to sit with her own arms resting on her lap—unresponsive to my touch.

Love—she still feels it. Thank you, God.

July 6, 1995
When I went to Welland today, I found Mom slumped over in her wheelchair asleep. She looked tired and didn't recognize me—not once today. She didn't even respond to my touch. I felt like a stranger to her—that she's all alone with no attachments to anyone. Her mind seems to be devoid of all thought. She's but a shell of her original self.

August 13, 1995
Mom is so ill. I believe she's got something seriously wrong with her. So far, they haven't found out what. The Lord is keeping me strong and I'm facing the possible loss of one of the dearest souls I've ever known. She has an eye infection, another discharge and a bed sore. She looks sick. From the time I arrived at 2:00 p.m., until 4:00 p.m., she had deteriorated considerably. I baked her favourite recipe, Lemon Supreme cake, for her birthday but she can't eat. Carl, Shirley, Trisha, Dad, Aunt Olive, Cameron and I were there with her. Aunt Violet and Uncle Scotty popped in. Most of the people who loved Mom were there, but she didn't seem to know any of us. She did smile.

Eventually, she had to be put to bed. Trish, at one point, commented, "Mom is still suffering in silence."

When I went back to check on her a little while later she was asleep and smiling. I wondered if God was comforting her with His promises.

August 15, 1995
Mom has been admitted to the hospital with extremely low potassium levels and a blood count so low she needs a transfusion. The nursing home staff has been neglectful. They did nothing as she deteriorated. Dr. L. (the doctor in emergency) said Mom's dehydrated. Why?— staff didn't give her enough to drink. It was discovered that they didn't record what she ate. Everyone is incompetent. Mom almost died! "The doctor in emergency was livid," said Shirley when I spoke to her later on in the day. He told her that Sunset Haven lets their patients dehydrate.

Mom's history was not sent with her to the hospital nor was her medication or any directive. The nursing home's attending doctor wouldn't examine her on Friday because she wasn't his patient.

Tonight when I phoned the hospital I was told that Mom was resting comfortably. The nurse on duty told me to call anytime. I'm anxiously waiting to see Mom tomorrow.

August 17, 1995
Melinda and I went to Welland yesterday. We arrived at 11 a.m. to be greeted with the news that Mom was under Dr. V. and therefore

under a new doctor who was helping him. I found Dr. S. to be pompous and arrogant. He contradicted himself on a number of things. Melinda witnessed it all. I was able to hold my own with him, letting him know I wasn't going to be intimidated. He was so smug and then, he discovered he had been talking to me about someone else—he had been referring to another patient's chart, thinking it was Mom's!

The day, in the end, was depressing. Mom is so sick. She can hardly speak and she's starting to get lesions on her body.

Mom continued to deteriorate over the next two weeks until she slipped into a coma.

September 3, 1995
As far as being strong in the Lord is concerned, it's amazing just how strong I feel. I know God will carry me through these difficult times. I'm thankful to be able to lean on Him and know that He is carrying me.

September 4 (11:35 p.m.) – Mom passed away at 9:32 p.m. as Trisha and I took turns holding her hand and wiping her eyes. They kept watering because she couldn't close them. Mom appeared to see nothing from the afternoon on. Her breathing became la-boured; her body was filling up with fluids indicating she was going into heart failure. Both Trisha and I were restless, moving about the room; sitting and standing up as Mom's breathing changed again. We waited until 8:30 p.m. and then, decided we should leave at 10:00 in order to have a good night's sleep know-ing that, on the next day, arrangements would have to be made for her funeral.

At one point, I went into the washroom and pleaded with the Lord to take her before we left. I couldn't bear the thought of Mom dying without one of us being there. When I returned to her room, the nurse told us her death would be soon—"only a few more respi-rations." There was no struggle or gasping—she just stopped breathing very slowly—quietly. Trish and I covered her body with our own bodies and wept together.

Soon after, I felt relief and an inner peace.

A little later, as I looked at my watch, I realized Craig turned forty-three today. What irony, it seemed to me, my mother would be taken to be with Jesus on Craig's birthday! Out of the 365 days in a year, God chose to bring Mom home on the birthday of the earthly son who had rejected her.

I realize now this wasn't irony. It was specific reassurance of God's very particular and continuing love for his child, Dora Brettell, born in Birmingham, England, eighty-seven years before. Regardless of the actions of one earthly son, God's Son lived and died for my mother. The sacrifice on the cross of God's Son had been for her, and she believed that he, Jesus, was the Christ.

For you created my inmost being; you knit me together in my mother's womb. I praise you because I am fearfully and wonderfully made; your works are wonderful, I know that full well. My frame was not hidden from you when I was made in the secret place. When I was woven together in the depths of the earth, your eyes saw my unformed body. All the days ordained for me were written in your book before one of them came to be (Psalm 139:13–16, NIV).

45

My dad, the clown

The Lord will not cast away weak saints for their great unbelief, because there is a little faith in them, or for their hypocrisy because of the little sincerity that is in them. Will the Lord cast away his dearest ones, because of their spots, blots and flaws? Surely no! God looks more upon the pearl, and not the spot in it. Well, remember this: the Lord Jesus has as great an interest in the weakest saints as the strongest.[33]

1995–1997

"I love you, Dad," I said as I zipped up my beige raincoat, preparing to leave.

Dad sat outside his room in his wheelchair, his legs crossed and head down. I spent a few hours with him that day.

Following Mom's death, I visited Dad every other week. He was less verbal now and more quietly agitated, constantly crossing and uncrossing his legs as he sat in his wheelchair. His back pain was ongoing, and although he was receiving medication for the pain, he often asked the nurses to put him to bed in order to give his aching back some relief.

"Why do you love me?" he asked.

I stood before him looking down at his bristly face. Reaching into my purse, I took out a Kleenex and wiped the chocolate from the corner of his mouth.

There were many reasons why I had come to love my Dad: the way he had taken care of me and showed me love when I was a little girl; the compassion he displayed for those who were hurting. I enjoyed his storytelling—his once keen memory for interesting items of news. None of these came to mind.

"I love you because you're funny!"

He looked up at me and smiled his toothless grin.

Dad said his dentures were stolen by two orderlies who came into his room during the night, held him down and pried both uppers and lowers from his mouth. He must have forgotten there were orderlies in the hospital, but not in the nursing home.

Oh Dad, did you go into the men's washroom and throw your teeth into the garbage? I won't ask you that out loud. You've always complained that those teeth were never a good fit. You've told me the dentist couldn't adjust them.

My dad didn't care that he looked like a toothless camel while chewing his food. In fact, the absence of his teeth became an opportunity for him to amuse the staff.

"Watch this," he'd say as the staff gathered together to give the residents their afternoon snacks. Dad would then suck in his lips, jut out his white-whiskered jaw and raise his chin up to meet his nose. As he had lost a considerable amount of weight during the last two years, his thin face and elongated nose helped with this achievement.

Ever since I could remember, he enjoyed making people laugh. And, he took particular pleasure in playing the clown to a captive audience.

Dad was both funny and smart. As long as he could see well— up until his early 80s—he continued to be a voracious reader. His mild dementia didn't impair his ability to spell.

The nurses used to brag about how he won all the spelling bees during patient activity time. You'd think it was their personal achievement, the way they would go on about him. I often wondered if my "whiz kid" dad was encouraging some heavy betting among the staff.

★ ★ ★ ★ ★

"Spell estimate," my daughter's fiancé, Tim, said to Dad once when Melinda and he were visiting. Melinda had told Tim about Grandpa's spelling bee successes.

"E-s-t-i-m-a-t-e."

"Spell severance," urged Tim.

"S-e-v-e-r-a-n-c-e."

For the next five minutes, Tim kept tossing out increasingly challenging words. "Spell supercalefragilisticexpealidocious."

"Go to hell!" Dad said, as he spun his wheelchair around and headed for his room.

Tim looked bewildered.

"I warned you not to mess with Grandpa," Melinda admonished.

★ ★ ★ ★ ★

In the last year of his life, Dad's most challenging health issues were constipation and recurring bouts of pneumonia. Although he was losing much of his ability to communicate, we could still engage in a superficial level of exchange.

"Dad," I said to him toward the end of one visit, "I know you're feeling terrible because your bowels haven't moved in several days, and the nurse is going to have to give you an enema which you hate. Would you like me to pray with you about it?"

He looked at me with raised eyebrows. Then, he turned away and gazed straight ahead as though waiting for me to make him a better offer.

Does he or doesn't he have faith in God and the power of prayer? Was he toying with me during those times of Bible study and discussion?

Dad didn't say, "Yes" but he didn't say, "No" either. So, I took his hand in mine, closed my eyes and asked God to relieve him of his discomfort.

When I opened my eyes, he sat staring at me.

"That's a lot of sh*t," he said.

For one brief moment, I thought of calling the nurse to give him an enema. Instead, I gave him a hug and squeezed his arm.

"I'll see you in two weeks, Dad."

"Yar," he responded.

What a character!

Visiting Mom and Dad in their room at Sunset Haven in the early nineties.

(from left) Claudia, Carl, Trisha, Scotty and Violet, Shirley. This photo was taken on May 28, 1997, following Dad's burial.

46

"Abide with me"

Even though I walk through the valley of the shadow of death, I will fear no evil, for you are with me; your rod and your staff they comfort me (Psalm 23:4, NIV).

On May 4, 1997—the night before Dad passed away from pneumonia—Melinda and I relieved Trisha, Shirley and Carl of their watch and continued the vigil with Dad until 12:30 a.m. He had slipped into unconsciousness before we arrived.

Together we took turns holding his hand and singing "Jesus Loves Me" many times over. Psalm 23 was printed on a wall plaque at the head of his bed. Hoping it would reach him, both Melinda and I read it aloud. Though he seemed unaware of our presence, we hoped if he could hear us, it would bring him some comfort.

After we said goodnight to the nursing staff, Melinda and I drove to a local hotel. We had asked the nurse not to notify us if he died during the night, as there would be much to do on the following day with respect to making funeral arrangements.

On May 5, I awoke at 7:00 a.m. and made the phone call.

"Your father passed away at 2:00 a.m.," said the nurse.

Although I expected it, I stood holding the phone for a few seconds before saying I would be right over to collect his belongings.

As Melinda and I walked toward the elevator, we met the night nurse coming off her shift.

"We're going to miss your Dad," she said as she took a tissue from her purse and blew her nose.

I tried to comfort her with a hug.

The loss of my father did not bring tears to my own eyes. I had forgiven him and learned to love him, but I remained confused by his multifaceted personality. He seemed to have more sides to him than a Rubik's Cube. I felt I had never fully known or understood him.

"Your Dad," the nurse said as she put her purse over her shoulder, "he was so much fun and so...religious."

"Religious?"

"Yes, he was always singing hymns. 'Abide with Me' seemed to be a favourite of his."

★ ★ ★ ★ ★

I came to the realization I had been trying to take on the job of the Holy Spirit. Rather than viewing myself as a conveyor of God's truth and letting the Holy Spirit work in and through Dad, I wanted his behaviour and his attitude to reveal an observable radical change—something like the one I experienced. I couldn't seem to accept that Dad might belong to God with all of his spots, blots and flaws.

Will the Lord cast away his dearest ones...?

Later on, I came to the conclusion I was probably just one of the many Christ-followers who influenced Dad over his ninety-two-year lifespan.

The seeds were planted—I had been there to add water.

★ ★ ★ ★ ★

Our family expected everything to run smoothly with respect to Dad's funeral. I called my cousin, Frances Brettell, who sang in the Anglican Church choir, and arranged for her to sing, "Abide with me."

The day before the funeral service, I received a phone call from Sandy, the director of the funeral home in Welland.

"We can't bury your father tomorrow. The ground is too soft.

We'll have to hold him here in the morgue until we're given the go-ahead at the cemetery."

"How long do you think it will be before that happens?"

"Oh, probably a week or so—I'll call you."

Three weeks later, I was still waiting.

On day twenty-two, the phone rang. I was told by Sandy that Dad had to be buried on the following day.

"Tomorrow? I don't know how I'll be able to get pallbearers on such short notice. Everyone will be working."

"Don't worry. We'll take care of all the details," he said.

I proceeded to phone my family to see who else could come to Welland with me for Dad's burial. As I suspected, few could make it on such short notice. I placed a call to Sandy and left a message on his voicemail. He didn't return my call.

Wednesday, May 28th was a warm, sunny spring day—the day of Shirley's birthday and Melinda's wedding anniversary. There we were, gathered together, all dressed up as though we were about to celebrate both.

The small group met in the parking lot of the funeral home. Mourners included Carl, Trisha, Shirley and Melinda, as well as my parents' two best friends, Violet and Scotty (who were well into their nineties), the Anglican minister, Rev. Thorpe, and me. Of the ten, I noticed only two men from the funeral home.

Ah, the others must be waiting at the cemetery.

Dad's casket was already in the hearse. We were told the order in which to follow the lead car, and then the procession began up the three city streets that led to the Smith Street cemetery where my mother was also buried.

As we slowly travelled the route, I noticed cars pulling over and stopping as our procession passed.

"Your grandfather would be beaming if he could witness the respect he is being given right now. Too bad it eluded him all of his life."

I took Melinda's hand in mine and continued to stare out the window.

My father's life had been bleak. However, not until after his death, did I ever try to look at things from his perspective. He had suffered from depression and chronic back pain and used alcohol as his elixir. To my knowledge, he never spoke of Craig once my brother severed ties with the family. I can only imagine how much emotional suffering he endured over the loss of his youngest son.

The complexity of his character kept me from truly knowing my father. I erected my own barriers at twelve years of age, when I discovered his love for the bottle. Surely, he was aware that my heart had grown cold toward him.

Never had I spent time reflecting on Dad's dismal life—only what he had done to me, to our family, to Mom. For many years, the walls I built around my unforgiving heart were fortified with feelings of justification. When the failure to forgive is held close to the chest, a person suffers as it eats away at their soul. The barriers to love are lifted with forgiveness. Christ's sacrifice on the cross released me from my burden of disdain.

Over the years, I grew in my faith as I read and memorized parts of Scripture. I came to realize it was God who gave me every opportunity to come to know him and to love him. I sought answers to difficult questions in his Word. He helped me understand what it meant to belong to him as his child.

For he chose us in him before the creation of the world to be holy and blameless in his sight. In love, He predestined us to be adopted as sons through Jesus Christ (Ephesians 1:4–5, NIV).

The minister greeted us as we got out of the car at the cemetery. He stood holding the Anglican *Book of Common Prayer* from which he would read for the committal of Dad's body.

Even though Dad rarely attended the Anglican Church, Rev. Thorpe, had conducted my mother's funeral and consented to conduct Dad's funeral when the time came.

Rev. Thorpe, a man in his mid-seventies, attired in his ecclesiastical robe, stood solemnly by the hearse as we waited for the pallbearers to remove Dad's casket.

Two men from the funeral home opened the back doors of the hearse as we all gathered around.

"Will the pallbearers please step forward for the carrying of the casket," said one of the men.

Silence.

I looked at Shirley who looked at Patricia. Patricia turned and looked at Carl, who looked at Melinda, who shrugged her shoulders and looked at me.

Melinda and I stepped forward in unison as though we had been rehearsing for this very moment.

There were now four pallbearers. We needed two more in addition to the two men from the funeral home.

Carl stepped forward next while Shirley and Trisha huddled together as though they were in the middle of an Alaskan deep freeze. Dad's two friends, Violet and Scotty, seemed to be taking it all in their stride.

When you get into your nineties, I suppose you've seen everything.

Rev. Thorpe handed his prayer book to Scotty and stepped forward to become the sixth pallbearer.

There we were, an unlikely group of pallbearers, gingerly stepping our way through the thick grass to Dad's place of burial.

A voice came from behind me.

"P-s-s-t. You're standing in the wrong place.

"Huh?" I said, fearful of falling if I turned around to see who was speaking

"His feet—they have to be the other way. You have the head where the feet should be," whispered the man from the funeral home.

"Together now, Melinda, we have to turn," I said.

"My heel's stuck."

"No, it's not! You're fine—move slowly."

I'm carrying my father to his final resting place. Would Dad be smiling at this little glitch, this little happenstance? Nothing happens by chance. I want to laugh—I can't cry—why can't I cry? Dad's gone—such an unfulfilled life. He's out of his misery—the hymn sung at his service—

Abide with me; fast falls the eventide;
  The darkness deepens; Lord with me abide.
When other helpers fail and comforts flee,
  Help of the helpless, O abide with me. [34]

Finally, we lowered the casket and set it down over Dad's grave. Rev. Thorpe turned to Scotty, who handed him back the prayer book, and he began—

For as much as it has pleased Almighty God of his great mercy to take unto himself our dear brother here departed: we, therefore, commit his body to the ground; earth to earth, ashes to ashes, dust to dust; in sure and certain hope of the resurrection to eternal life, through our Lord Jesus Christ; who shall change our corruptible body, that it may be like unto his glorious body, according to the mighty working whereby he is able to subdue all things to himself. Amen.[35]

* * * * *

My doctor's appointment, on Bloor Street in downtown Toronto, came on a sticky, humid summer day in July 1997—two months after my father's death.

As I walked down the street toward the office building, I noticed an elderly man with a walker shuffling along several metres ahead of me. His head was lowered and as I approached him, I could see his grey hair sticking straight out at the nape of his neck. Its texture appeared to be much like Dad's—thin and stringy.

As I was about to pass, he turned toward me. He looked to be in his late eighties—a clear-eyed man with stooped posture and many wrinkles. He was neatly dressed in trousers and a long-sleeved cotton shirt.

"Can you spare some money so I can buy a cup of coffee, miss?"

I fumbled with my purse to undo the clasp. The first thing I touched was a tissue.

Good—I have a Kleenex! Other than having the same hair texture, this man doesn't resemble Dad in the slightest. Why am I thinking about my father?

I sniffed as I finally found my wallet and handed the man a bill.

"Thank you, miss."

I nodded and returned his smile.

As I continued to walk down the street, I pulled out the Kleenex and clutched it in my damp hand. My chin began to quiver; a heaviness pressed upon my chest. Seconds later, tears began to trickle down my cheeks.

★ ★ ★ ★ ★

Although the relationship with my earthly father still contains many mysteries, the relationship I have with my heavenly Father is a vibrant, loving one. He grants the peace and joy my earthly father was unable to give.

Endnotes

1 "Show Me the Way To Go Home" is a folk song believed to be of English origin. It was made famous by its 1925 adaptation by the pseudonymous "Irving King" (the British song-writing team of James Campbell and Reginald Connelly).

2 *The Ed Sullivan Show*, an American TV variety show (first titled, *Toast of the Town*), ran from June 20, 1948 until June 6, 1971.

3 *Creature from the Black Lagoon* was a 1954 monster horror film.

4 "Be-Bop-A-Lula" was recorded by Gene Vincent in May 1956.

5 Max Haines, "Crime Flashback," *Ottawa Citizen* (June 25, 1983): "On Jan. 16, 1958, LaPlante ate a chicken dinner at the Welland County Jail and said, 'See ya, boys,' to fellow inmates, and walked unaided to the gallows. The words were ironic, for after the execution, it was revealed that Tommy LaPlante had left his eyes to the Ontario Eye Bank.

6 William H. Lewis, *Aqueduct, Merrittville and Welland: A History of the City of Welland*, Volume 3: *The 20th Century* (Welland: AMW Publications, n.d.), 195. Welland's modern traffic problems may have started the day the newly-completed Main Street liftbridge was opened to vehicular traffic. On April 30, 1930, *The Tribune* editorialized that the new bridge "has brought with it new problems—in traffic control."

7 Sidney Katz, "Going Steady: Is It Ruining Our Teenagers?" *Maclean's* (January 3, 1959), in *Canada's Golden Decade: From The Achives of Maclean's* (Toronto: Penguin, 1999), 135.

8 *I've Got a Secret* was a panel game show that ran from 1952 until 1967.

9 Proverbs 12:22.

10 Hurricane Hazel hit on October 15, 1954: "It was a gigantic flood with smashed houses and uprooted trees bobbing like corks, everything going down the river so fast..." Bryan Mitchell, volunteer firefighter, *Toronto Star* (October 14, 1984).

11 Released in 1961, "Town Without Pity" was Gene Pitney's first hit. The song (from a movie by the same name) won the first Golden Globe award for best original song (Source: Songfacts).

12 "Whole Lotta Shakin' Goin' On" is a song best known for the 1957 rock and roll/ rockabilly hit version by Jerry Lee Lewis.

13 "The House of the Rising Sun" was recorded by The Animals in 1964.

14 "Only the Lonely (Know the Way I Feel)" was released in June 1960. Written by Roy Orbison, it became his first major hit.

15 W.M. Hutchings, "When Mothers of Salem,"in *The Book of Common Prayer being The Hymn Book of The Anglican Church of Canada*, 281.

16 "Aquarius/Let the Sunshine In" from the musical *Hair*, was a 1969 hit made popular by the Fifth Dimension.

17 The Electric Circus was a trendy nightclub opened in 1968 on Queen Street in Toronto. Strobe lights were used and people could dance while the music played.

18 "The Communion"in *Book of Common Prayer – Hymn Book*, 282.

19 *Book of Common Prayer – Hymn Book*, 266

20 W. Kuipers, *Book of Praise, Anglo-Genevan Psalter* (revised; 1931), Psalm 116.

21 W. van der Kamp, *Book of Praise, Anglo-Genevan Psalter* (revised; 1972), Hymn 48:1.

22 Clem Kadiddlehopper was a character played by Red Skelton, a comedian, on *The Red Skelton Show*. Skelton's variety show ran from 1951 until 1971.

23 Matthew Mead, "A Name in Heaven," in Richard Rushing, ed., *Voices from the Past: Puritan Devotional Readings* (Edinburgh: Banner of Truth, 2009), 77–103.

24 Psalm 119:105.

25 Hebrews 13:5.

26 Helen Duff Baugh established The Christian Business Women's Council of America in 1938 as a dinner program where the gospel of Jesus Christ was presented to career women in cities across America. In 1948, Mary E. Clark joined Baugh to help lead the rapidly growing evangelistic and missionary organization. In 1952, the ministry's international headquarters relocated to the Stonecroft land in Kansas City, Missouri, and the group of outreach ministries took on the property's name. The mission of Stonecroft Ministries (Christian Womens' Clubs of Canada) is to equip and encourage women to impact their communities with the gospel of Jesus Christ (https://www.stonecroft.org/ home/about).

27 George Swinnock, *Works*, 1:27–45, quoted in Rushing, ed., *Voices from the Past.*

28 William Gurnall, *The Christian in Complete Armour*, 11:91–97, quoted in Rushing, ed., *Voices from the Past.*

29 Carol Kent is a popular international speaker. She is founder and director of Speak Up with Confidence seminars.

30 1 Thessalonians 5:17.

31 Andrew Murray, *The Power of Persevering Prayer*, in *Andrew Murray: Collected Works on Prayer – 7 Books in 1* (New Kensington: Whitaker House, 2013), 554.

32 Philippians 4:7.

33 Thomas Brooks, *Works*, 111:62–63, quoted in Rushing, ed., *Voices from the Past.*

34 "Abide with Me" was written by Henry Francis Lyte in 1847.

35 "At the Burial of the Dead" in *Book of Common Prayer – Hymn Book*, 377.

Other titles available from Joshua Press...

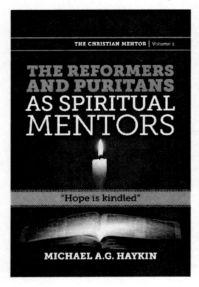

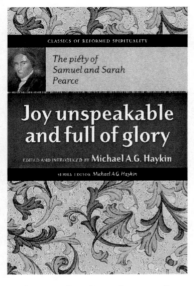

The Christian Mentor | Volume 2

The reformers and Puritans as spiritual mentors
"Hope is kindled"

By Michael A.G. Haykin

REFORMERS SUCH as Tyndale, Cranmer and Calvin, and Puritans Richard Greenham, John Owen, etc. are examined to see how their display of the light of the gospel provides us with models of Christian conviction and living.

ISBN 978–1-894400–39–8

Classics of Reformed spirituality

Joy unspeakable and full of glory
The piety of
Samuel and Sarah Pearce

By Michael A.G. Haykin

SAMUEL PEARCE played a key role in the formation and early days of the Baptist Missionary Society in eighteenth-century England. Through Samuel and Sarah's letters we are given a window into their rich spiritual life and living piety.

ISBN 978–1-894400–48–0

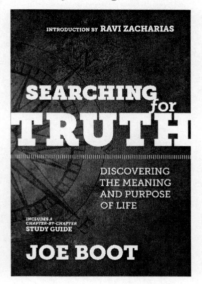

The grace of godliness

An introduction to doctrine and piety in the Canons of Dort

By Matthew Barrett

BARRETT opens a window on the synod's deliberations with the Remonstrants and examines the main emphases of the canons, with special attention on their relationship to biblical piety and spirituality.

ISBN 978-1-894400-52-7 (PB)

Searching for truth

Discovering the meaning and purpose of life

By Joe Boot

BEGINNING WITH a basic understanding of the world, Joe Boot explains the biblical worldview, giving special attention to the life and claims of Jesus Christ. He wrestles with questions about suffering, truth, morality and guilt.

ISBN 978-1-894400-40-4

Deo Optimo et Maximo Gloria
To God, best and greatest, be glory

www.joshuapress.com

CPSIA information can be obtained at www.ICGtesting.com
Printed in the USA
BVOW02s0322250316

441584BV00005B/6/P